—THE ART OF—
MYSTERY
& DETECTIVE
STORIES

THE ART OF
MYSTERY
& DETECTIVE
STORIES

THE BEST ILLUSTRATIONS FROM OVER
A CENTURY OF CRIME FICTION

PETER HAINING
Designed by Christopher Scott

TREASURE PRESS

For
A. POXONIT
– and all friends
of the Restoration

First published in Great Britain in 1977 by
Souvenir Press Ltd under the title *Mystery*

This edition published in 1986 by
Treasure Press
59 Grosvenor Street
London W1

ISBN 1 85051 135 7

Printed in Portugal by
Oficinas Gráficas ASA

CONTENTS

INTRODUCTION

The popularity of crime and detective fiction is one of the indis-
putable facts of literature, and whether a reader's interest in the
genre is just casual, or taken to the degree that he will engage in
the most involved arguments about some minor point of theory
concerning the Sherlock Holmes cases, the entertainment and
enjoyment that can be drawn from them is beyond question.
Howard Haycraft, the American critic who wrote one of the first —
and still among the best — studies of the genre, *Murder For
Pleasure* (1942), was in no doubt about how widespread this
appeal was. 'It is a matter of sober statistical record,' he wrote,
'that one out of every four new works of fiction published in the
English language belongs to this category, while the devotion the
form has managed to rouse in millions of men and women in all
walks of life, the humble and the eminent, has become a latter-
day legend.'

Inspector Field, the London policeman
who was a close friend of Charles
Dickens and provided the famous
novelist with much information about
crime and criminals. Dickens wrote an
article about his friend, 'On Duty With
Inspector Field', which was published
with this illustration by E. G. Dalziel in
Household Words in 1860.

The two most famous English detectives — and perhaps the most famous in the world: Sherlock Holmes and Sexton Blake. The Holmes portrait is by the great detective's best-known illustrator, Sidney Paget, while the Blake picture is by one of the many unknown artists who portrayed the sleuth for his publishers, Fleetway Publications. **(Below)** One of the favourite scenes from Victorian detective fiction — the moment the murderer strikes! Lancelot Speed was the artist who drew this picture for Robert Barr's crime series, 'Tales of Revenge' in *The English Illustrated Magazine*, 1893.

It is an extraordinary success story — made all the more extraordinary by the fact that the genre is only a little over a century and a quarter old. There are, of course, cases advanced that mystery stories of a kind are to be found in the Bible (the verses on 'Bel and the Dragons' and 'Susanna' in the Apocrypha section) and among ancient documents from China and the East, not to mention tales from Asia, Africa and the traditions of the Indians of North America and Canada. But none of these are really fiction, and though containing the required elements of a mystery being solved by reason, have always been understood to be based on fact. A better case does exist over the stories of the tracking skill of the Indians, and indeed it is more than likely that early detective story writers used such legends, relocated in urban settings, as a basis for many mysteries.

No, the story really begins with that writer of genius, Edgar Allan Poe, who with three stories of a detective, Auguste Dupin, and three more of varying degrees of 'detective' work, provided the formula on which virtually all subsequent stories in the genre are based. The appearance of those tales, in the 1840s, saw the beginnings of this literary form which today embraces the world.

The genre now goes under many names — the *Roman Policier* in France, the *Kriminalroman* in Germany, for example — and may well enjoy its appeal everywhere because, as G. K. Chesterton has suggested, it is the only form of popular literature 'in which is expressed some sense of the poetry of modern life'. H. Douglas Thomson, who wrote the first study of the form, *Masters of Mystery* in 1931, has, however, gone further in his analysis. 'Perhaps you regard the public craze for detective stories as but another example of the rabid delight in sensationalism which is said to be characteristic of our age. Or you may be slightly more magnaminous and descry it the lesser of two unfortunate evils — an escape from fiction's obsession in sex problems. Again you may favour a more positive criticism, and regard the detective story as a tonic for jaded nerves, or a means for dispelling the tediousness of a journey.' Mr Thomson sees the story itself in the clearest possible light — 'what is the detective story if not a grown-up nonsense rather proud of its education and logic?'

WARWICK
REYNOLDS

In essence, though, the detective story is primarily the solution of a problem, and the reader has two alternatives when approaching such a work. He may regard it simply as a story and await the outcome in its own good time — or he may pit his own wits against those of the author and attempt to unravel the mystery before he is presented with the solution. That for me, and I know for many others, is the beginning and the end of the matter.

Despite the shortness of its history, the crime and detective story has come in for more than its fair share of study, both popular and scholarly. Books on Sherlock Holmes alone, for instance, would now fill a small library, and those on Poe and the other important figures in the genre lag not far behind. It has been wryly observed — and not without a certain amount of truth — that we are in danger of obscuring the purpose of the story with too much analysis. Yet, this said, why another book on the genre? The answer is simple — in my opinion not enough attention has been paid to the illustrations and illustrators who played an important — not to say crucial — part in the development of the mystery story. The early images of the detectives presented in the magazines and books in which they appeared played a major part in their subsequent success. For example, no Sherlockian needs a clearer demonstration of this fact than to recall how much the early Holmes owed to his great illustrator, Sidney Paget.

It is for this reason, then, that *Mystery!* has been assembled — drawing on pictures from the time of Poe's inception of the detective story to the advent of World War II. I have not gone beyond this date for two reasons. First, there have been no further major developments in the genre since that date (I discount the spy story as really being beyond the scope of a work such as this); and second, few modern detective stories are given more than an illustration on their dust-jackets, so I believe the reader would feel

justifiably annoyed at being asked to pay for reproductions of covers he probably already has on his shelves. Sadly, publishing economics have made illustrations inside new books impossible — and perhaps the very popularity of the genre has made those who purvey it feel that such niceties are a pointless exercise anyway.

To be fair, I must add that the keen-eyed reader will find one or two important authors from the more recent periods not represented among these pages. (As my own little mystery, you will have to find out which ones for yourself!) In these cases they were originally unillustrated, or there were no suitable pictures available for one reason or another. I hope, too, that as over the years something like 10,000 writers have produced crime and detective stories, I may be forgiven if a few personal favourites are also found to be missing. What I have tried to achieve — drawing primarily on magazines, with books a secondary source — is a general history of the genre utilising those pictures which best illustrate its major developments and important characters. I have sought out and found the leading detectives, their assistants and adversaries, and even special moments from their best cases. I do not for one moment claim the book to be exhaustive, but it is a fair reflection of the development and plumps unashamedly for visual excitement and drama when in doubt. I particularly commend many of the artists to you: most are men long forgotten in public memory and undeservedly so.

It was Nicholas Blake who wrote not so long ago that he considered the detective 'the Fairy Godmother of the twentieth-century folk-myth, his magic capabilities only modified to the requirements of a would-be scientific and rational generation.' That he is capable of weaving a spell over the world's readers we have established beyond doubt — I trust the pictures in the pages which follow will also give visual form to this special magic as well.

The private eye or 'Hardboiled Dick' as personified in the pulp magazines. This composite illustration **(top left)** was by Joseph Doolin for *Clues Magazine*, 1932. The private eyes fought all manner of villains in the pages of the pulps — two of the most popular were the 'Master Criminal' as shown on the cover of *Crime Mysteries* (1934) painted by Samuel Cahan, and the 'Yellow Peril' or fiendish Oriental as illustrated by Tom Lovell for *Detective Tales* (1936).

2. THE ANNALS
OF NEWGATE

(Page ten) Earliest known illustration of law officers making an arrest for murder based on the 'detection' of the criminal — from *The Annals of Newgate* by the Reverend John Villette (1776).

(Facing page) (Top) Eighteenth-century engraving of a public execution at Newgate.
(Bottom) One of the first engravings of an organised criminal gang — led by the notorious Levi Weil — committing a robbery at Chelsea, from *The Newgate Calendar Improved* by George Wilkinson (1816).
(Top) Gruesome illustration of Mary Aubrey murdering her husband — also from Wilkinson's *The Newgate Calendar Improved*.
(Above) Law officers torturing a suspect for information from *The New & Complete Newgate Calendar* by William Jackson (1818).

The fiction which most amused our ancestors was a study in rascality; and before our fiction began, our most popular ballads concerned the homicides and robberies of Robin Hood.

H. DOUGLAS THOMSON
Masters of Mystery: A Study of the Detective Story

The literary origins of the crime and detective story can be found in the famous series of Newgate *Calendars* or *Annals* which reported unusual crimes in graphic prose and lurid woodcuts. For many years the confessions of criminals and their dying speeches had provided highly lucrative material for the sellers of broadsheets and chapbooks, but in 1776 a chaplain at the notorious Newgate prison in London decided there was enough material in the cells and prison blocks all around him to fill more than one book, let alone a broadsheet.

This man was the Reverend John Villette, described as 'The Ordinary Chaplain' who published the results of his contacts with murderers, robbers, rapists, thieves and other sundry criminals as *The Annals of Newgate; or, The Malefactor's Register*. The work appeared in four volumes, complete with over thirty copperplate engravings of the more distinguished malefactors in the process of carrying out their violent and bloody crimes. Reverend Villette's book was expensive and way beyond the means of the common people; publishers soon put this to rights with weekly penny issues detailing 'Newgate Crimes' of all kinds. (When the more unscrupulous ran out of factual material, they merely had their writers invent still more gruesome and sensational accounts!)

Despite the catch-penny Newgate stories, there were later volumes composed by writers of ability and it is these — such as the works of Wilkinson (1816), Jackson (1818) and Knapp and Baldwin (1824), along with those of Villette himself — that are represented on these next pages. The influence of these works, it must be added, was far-reaching. Many of the contemporary Gothic novel writers drew details and even plots from the stories, and crime and detective writers in later generations were to turn eagerly to their pages — and illustrations — in the search for inspiration and period details. They even gave rise to what became known as 'Newgate novels' featuring such 'heroes' as Dick Turpin, Jack Shepherd, *et al*. Today, still, they present a vivid insight into crime and punishment at the start of an important era.

Three illustrations from probably the most famous *Newgate Calendar* by Andrew Knapp and William Baldwin, both attorneys-at-law (1824). Matthew Clarke, a seducer and murderer of young women who was finally caught by bloodstains detected on his coat.

William Johnson shooting a law officer in the Old Bailey where his mistress, Jane Housden, is on trial for forgery. Both were later hanged for murder.

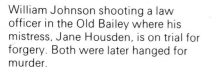

The *real* Dick Turpin — the vicious and unscrupulous highwayman thrusting an old woman on the fire to reveal the whereabouts of her money.

Penny-weekly issues of *The New Newgate Calendar* (1864) sold in enormous numbers and the publishers included as much fiction as fact in each issue. In the top illustration a 'Peeler' observes a masked burglar attacking his victim.
(Right) A group of 'Peelers' rounding up a gang of criminals in a highly dramatic situation.

3. THE FATHER OF THE DETECTIVE STORY

(Previous page) A superb picture for Poe's *The Mystery of Marie Roget* from the first illustrated edition in the world of the author's works, published by Clarke Beeton, London, 1851. The illustrator is unknown. An outstanding colour illustration of the world's first detective, Auguste Dupin, revealing the mystery of *The Murders in the Rue Morgue* and drawn by Byam Shaw in 1909.

(Above) The first picture of the first detective — Poe's brilliant amateur criminologist Auguste Dupin listens to the baffled Prefect of Police who is trying to solve the murder of the young girl in *The Mystery of Marie Roget* (Clarke Beeton edition, 1851).

(Right) Marie Roget serving perfume in M. Le Blanc's shop.

No student of crime and detective fiction needs telling of the paramount importance to the genre of the works of Edgar Allan Poe (1809–49), the tormented genius of American letters who left his pen mark indelibly on so many areas of literature. For Poe literally invented the detective story as we know it today, providing, as Howard Haycraft says, a virtual vade-mecum in a few thousand words. He gave us the first fictional detective, C. Auguste Dupin, too, and – as Dorothy L. Sayers has further noted – 'taken all around, *The Murders in the Rue Morgue* constitutes in itself almost a complete manual of detective theory and practice'.

There is no necessity to repeat the details of Poe's wretched existence here, only to say that the failures of his life have been compensated in death by his being placed at the very pinnacle of literature, and his work kept in print in every major language of the world. It is in his detective stories that we are interested – and there are only three of them: *The Murders in the Rue Morgue* (written in 1841), *The Mystery of Marie Roget* (1842) and *The Purloined Letter* (1844), all featuring Dupin. To be fair, *The Gold Bug* (1843) has been described as 'the best detective story ever written', but it is rather the story of the solution of a cipher which leads to buried treasure; and *Thou Art The Man* (1844) and *The Man In The Crowd* (1845) also put forward in this category are only marginally concerned with any form of 'detection'. Yet it would be churlish to deny that with these six tales Poe has provided the elements on which nine-tenths of all subsequent detective stories have been based.

It is interesting to note that Poe did not once use the term 'detective' in his stories – to him they were tales of 'ratiocination' – and it is unlikely that he would have written even the stories he did if there were not already police forces in operation on both sides of the Atlantic. (Those famous pioneers the 'Peelers' or 'Bobbies' had been in existence in England since 1814, and by the 1840s were being referred to more respectfully as 'detective police'.)

The reason why Poe should have set his detective stories in Paris when he had never been there (although there are unsubstantiated rumours to the contrary) is simply that he had been influenced by the stories of the French criminal-cum-detective Vidocq whose *Mémoires* had been published to sensational acclaim when Poe was a young man (see next section). On the other hand, the reason why he should have tried this form of story when he was already charting out new territory in the weird and the macabre is more difficult to explain. Perhaps Joseph Krutch's statement is worth more than a passing thought, 'Poe invented the detective story that he might not go mad.'

(Above) The third of Poe's stories featuring Auguste Dupin in which he discovers 'The Purloined Letter' almost literally under the noses of everyone.
(Below) 'Thou Art The Man' in which the least likely person proves to be the villain!

(Above and facing page) Poe's first story featuring the detective Auguste Dupin in which he brilliantly solves the horrific *Murders in the Rue Morgue*.

(Left) Another anonymous artist's illustration for Poe's *The Man of the Crowd*, which contains the first instance of a person thought to be a criminal being 'shadowed'.

(Below) Two pictures from the 1851 publication of *The Gold Bug* in which Poe recounts how 'detective' William Legrand deciphers a code and discovers hidden treasure.

4. LE ROMAN POLICIER

(Previous page) The French detective Eugène Vidocq searching for clues at the scene of a murder — an illustration from *Life In Paris* (1848).

(Facing page) A series of illustrations from the English edition of Vidocq's biography *Life and Adventures* (1841). Vidocq's youthful thefts from his father's shop lead to prison from which he unsuccessfully tries to escape naked! Further narrow escapes from the law while in a brothel and then disguised as a guard, lead to his joining the police, and following his first arrest of an escaping forger he progresses to great triumphs, particularly in the Paris underworld which he once frequented.

(Above) Title page of *Life in Paris* (1848) and W. Boucher's picture of Vaturin, a character whom Balzac based on Vidocq for his book *Old Gorot*.

It was necessary that a Vidocq should issue his Mémoires *for the literary transition from rogue to detective to be definitely effected.*
FRANK W. CHANDLER
The Literature of Roguery

The French influence on Edgar Allan Poe's pioneer detective stories is undisputed, though the work of one man, the roguish Eugene François Vidocq, was perhaps the most important. The experiences of this 'French Jonathan Wilde', as he was called, had been related in his extraordinary *Mémoires* published in 1827 with enormous success. There was obviously a good deal of fiction interwoven with the 'facts' of Vidocq's life during the epoch of the French Revolution, in which he described his career from being a boy thief to criminal gang-leader and then, finally, a prince of thief-takers for the Sûreté Générale. Howard Haycraft, the crime historian, has even gone so far as to suggest that if Vidocq himself wrote all the 'stories' contained in the book then he, rather than Poe, might be looked upon as the actual inventor of the detective story!

What there can be no question about is that Vidocq inspired a whole new generation of writers not only in his own country, but in Britain and America as well. His most important disciple in France was Emile Gaboriau (1832–73), a frustrated soldier who turned to eeking out a meagre living writing snippets for newspapers, and then created Monsieur Lecoq, the Sûreté detective who became an international favourite. As Gaboriau's works took the form of full-length novels, he is looked upon in many quarters as the 'Father of the Detective *Novel*', as distinct from Poe whose work was confined to the short story. In introducing his famous book, *L'Affaire Lerouge* (1866), Gaboriau explained how he had evolved his work. 'In reading the memoires of celebrated police agents I became inspired by an enthusiastic admiration for these men so untiring in pursuit, so fertile in expedient, who follow crime to its stronghold as relentlessly as the savages of Cooper pursue their enemies in the depths of the American forest.'

While Gaboriau's novels were to become the best known of the *Romans Policiers* — as books in the genre were styled — others were to make important contributions. Ponson du Terrail (1829–71), a prolific writer of adventure stories, created Rocambole, a street urchin who graduated from being a thief to a brilliant amateur detective. Like Conan Doyle at a later period, du Terrail became tired of his creation's popularity and tried to kill him off — only to be forced to resurrect him in the ensuing outcry! Fortune du Boisgobey (1824–91) also enjoyed considerable popularity in this field — many of his sensational novels being translated into English — but he is perhaps best remembered for having appropriated Gaboriau's character Lecoq and making him the hero of *The Old Age of Lecoq* without so much as a by-your-leave to his creator! Such was the success of these *Romans Policiers* that it is perhaps not surprising to find that some of the most important French novelists of the period, such as Eugène Sue and Honoré de Balzac, also wrote a few mystery stories.

Such was the next step in our history as it occurred in France. The reasons for its growth here are perhaps not easy to define, but H. Douglas Thomson in his study strikes one as being closest: 'An explanation of this might be found in the unfailing attraction the *crime passionel* has for the Gallic temperament, but we shall have to leave it at that.'

25

(Above) Prince Rodolphe, the hero of Eugène Sue's serial story *The Mysteries of Paris* (1842–43), who lives in the underworld battling crime.
(Right) A dramatic scene by W. Boucher for Balzac's crime novel *The Gonderville Mystery*, in which the authorities become the villains by having innocent people found guilty.
(Far right) The adventurer-cum-private-detective Rocambole created by Ponson du Terrail, who was the forerunner of long-running serials such as Sexton Blake and Nick Carter. His adventures from 1855 to 1870 roamed through many locations and the most extraordinary incidents and escapes.
(Above right) Another highly popular French author, Fortuné du Boisgobey, whose crime stories were notable for their authenticity. Over thirty were translated into English. He also created M. Jean, a kindly old curé and detective in the Father Brown mould.

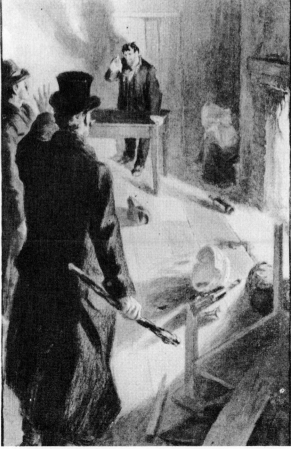

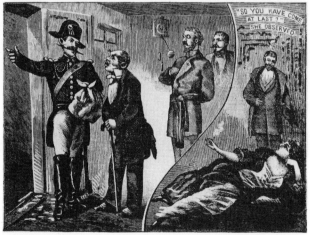

A page of pictures illustrating the international popularity of Emile Gaboriau, the most important of the *Roman Policier* authors.

(Left) Gaboriau's famous detective Monsieur Lecoq in disguise and confronting a dangerous criminal, in drawings by Bayard Jones for *Monsieur Lecoq* 1901.

(Above) The discovery of the body of *The Widow Lerouge* pictured by Louise Heustis (1902); and an anonymous American 'dime novel' engraving for '*Piping' The Lerouge Case* (*Old Cap Collier Library*, 1883).

5. CRIME IN THE PENNY BLOODS

(Previous page) The heroine finds
the wounded body of her husband — a
typical 'fierce' engraving from the
famous 'Penny Blood' *Grace Rivers; or
The Merchant's Daughter* by Thomas
Prest (1844).

(Top left) Another anonymous
engraving from *Grace Rivers*, of a
masked robber at work. Illustrations
like these appeared on the first page of
each weekly issue.

(Above) A 'Penny Blood' based on a
famous eighteenth-century criminal
case in Suffolk, *Susan Hoply; or, The
Trials and Vicissitudes of a Servant Girl*
by Thomas Prest (1841). The work
was actually a plagiarism of Mrs
Catherine Crowe's work, *Adventures
of Susan Hoply*, published in book
form the same year.

(Left) The continuing interest in crime
stories emanating from Newgate was
exemplified by Thomas Prest's long-
running serial *Newgate*, which ran for
97 weeks in 1846–47 and contained a
great deal of fiction to keep reader
interest alive!

(Opposite) Another 'Penny Blood'
based on a real character, *George
Barrington, The Gentleman
Pickpocket*, who was transported to
Australia in 1791 for his crimes.
Thomas Frost wove this romance
around his exploits — and many
imaginary ones — and it enjoyed
enormous success (1852). Barrington,
for his part, actually turned from crime
in Australia and was responsible for
introducing the first theatrical perfor-
mance in the colony!

While the crucial developments in the genre were being made by Poe in America and Gaboriau and his compatriots in France, crime stories were also finding an ever-increasing readership in Britain — primarily among the buyers of the weekly serials known as 'Penny Bloods'. These strikingly illustrated, often atrociously written, but always vivid and sensational tales were published to catch any public fancy and lived or died totally dependent on their sales. The writers who produced the eight-page issues — complete with the most eye-catching engraving publisher and artist could devise — were under constant orders to pack as much drama and bloodshed into each as they could; and if sales flagged they would have to wind up the story, which might be immensely complicated, in a single issue!

The publishers of these 'Penny Bloods', headed by men like Edward Lloyd, John Dicks and William Clark, were hardheaded and unscrupulous, playing on the unsophisticated minds of their readers, fully aware that the most unlikely twists and turns in a plot for the sake of expediency would not cause the slightest murmur of protest. Sometimes even the pictures had little to do with the story! It is interesting looking at these publications today to see that the first line of each new issue continues immediately from the preceding one without so much as a word of explanation, and it is by no means uncommon to find an episode ending in mid-sentence at the bottom of page eight! It would continue with the next word in the following issue under the dramatic illustration as if nothing untoward had happened at all!

The writers of the 'Bloods' are mostly now forgotten men, poor hacks who ground out millions of words for a mere pittance, and with a few notable exceptions died in the most unhappy circumstances. The most successful of these authors was probably George W. M. Reynolds (1814–79) who began by plagiarising Dickens and then protected his own popularity by holding a stake in the magazine which published him. An early influence was the Frenchman Eugène Sue, and Reynolds took up the idea of his *Mysteries of Paris* and wrote *The Mysteries of the Court* (1849) which contained several crime stories and the appearance of one of the earliest Bow Street Runners as a hero, Grumley. Thomas Prest (1810–79) enjoyed similar popularity to Reynolds for some years, but dissipated his earnings and eventually died in wretched circumstances. Prest was an expert at weaving 'Bloods' around famous crime stories. He wrote the first fictionalised version of the Sweeney Todd legend and added to the already voluminous shelf of books about Newgate. Much of Prest's work was published by Edward Lloyd, as was Thomas Frost (1801–79), another expert noveliser of stories of crime and mystery, who later became so disenchanted with his work that he took up writing religious tracts! The section is completed with examples of the work of the prolific Edward Ellis (1814–80) who wrote some early novels about spying, and created a remarkable youthful hero, 'The Boy Detective', perhaps the earliest of his kind.

(Top) The criminal fraternity of London at all levels of society were vividly portrayed in G. W. M. Reynolds' serial *The Mysteries of the Court of London*, published in 1849. Henry Anelay drew these pictures of the Bow Street Runner Grumley investigating a suicide, and a hapless victim about to be sealed up alive in the walls of a building under construction. Shades of some recent crime reports!

(Right) *Rosa Lambert*, the unfortunate heroine of G. W. N. Reynolds' serial of the same name, was subjected to all manner of crimes including this attack by a rapist. Frederick Gilbert was the artist (1854).

(Facing page) First page of Edward Ellis' popular underworld serial, *Rook the Robber; or, London Fifty Years Ago*, published in 1860.

ROOK THE ROBBER;

OR,

LONDON FIFTY YEARS AGO.

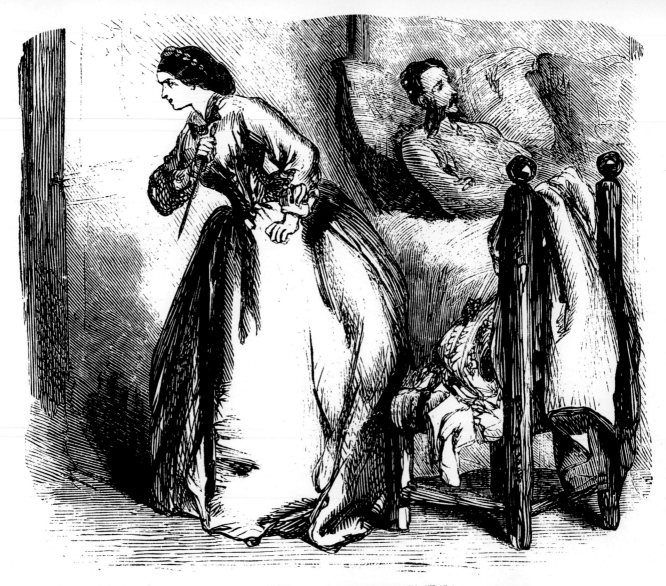

One of the rarest and most unusual of all 'Penny Blood' serials, *Ruth The Betrayer; or, The Female Spy* by Edward Ellis (1863). Ruth operated on both sides of the law and was often in trouble with both. W. H. Thwaites illustrated her escape from a sleeping victim after she has obtained the required information, and in a tricky situation when accosted by a policeman.

Perhaps the rarest of all 'Penny Dreadfuls' — the juvenile successors to the 'Penny Bloods' — *The Boy Detective or, The Crimes of London*, published about 1860. The lurid woodcuts on the first page of each instalment traced the bizarre but courageous exploits of this young man who hunted down and brought to justice villains of all kinds.

(Top) The Boy Detective is captured by the unscrupulous 'Queen of the Coiners', leader of a gang of forgers.

(Middle) He rescues a scantily clad and securely bound girl from a burning house: appropriately she becomes his girlfriend.

(Bottom) Unafraid, the brave youngster arrests a cunning and dangerous master criminal. The author of this remarkable pioneer detective story, which predates a whole school of youthful heroes, was Edward Ellis.

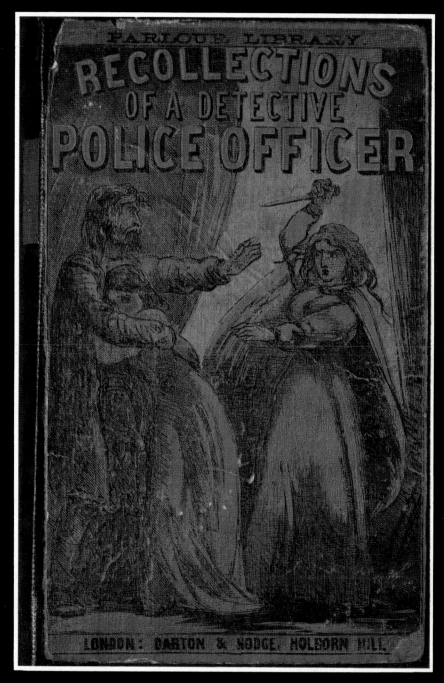

Illustrated above is a rare edition with
coloured front cover of one of the
earliest true detective stories,
*Recollections of a Detective Police-
Officer* by 'Waters', a pseudonym of
William Russell, a novelist of the
Victorian era about whom virtually
nothing is known. Yet his collection of
tales about the exploits of the clever
'Detective Police Officer', are among
the most important in the history of
crime fiction.

6. THE OPENING OF THE CASE...

past, but demonstrates himself an outstanding and successful investigator.

(Below) Charles Dickens played an important part in the development of the detective story and was the first novelist to show the police force in a favourable light. This illustration by E. G. Dalziel is for *The Sofa* in which a Sergeant Dornton, his face covered by a handkerchief, creeps out from his hiding-place to catch a pick-pocket red-handed (1870).

(Bottom) Another important figure at this time was Wilkie Collins and this engraving, also by Dalziel, was for his mystery story 'The Yellow Mask' which appeared in his collection, *After Dark* (1856).

In the years that followed the formation of the first detective police force in London, an immense popularity was achieved by those writers who wrote detective fiction novels and works devoted to criminal investigation.
ERIC QUAYLE
The Collector's Book of Detective Fiction

Aside from the 'Penny Bloods', there were more substantial contributions to the developing detective story genre being made in Britain during the middle years of the nineteenth century. As in France, there appeared a number of works based on 'true recollections' of former police officers, which were to spawn their own imitators and indeed a considerable number of detective tales. The first of these was the remarkable *Scenes in the Life of a Bow Street Runner* by an author known only as 'Richmond' and published in 1827. Hailed as the first such work of its kind, the book recounts a group of cases successfully solved by the Bow Street Runners, the special group of law officers attached to Bow Street Court who had been operating since the previous century and tackled a variety of crimes.

After 'Richmond', two Scottish authors made significant contributions to the genre with works which are now extremely rare collectors' items. The first was Angus Reach (1821–56), the son of an Inverness solicitor, who had a short, ill-fated career as a journalist, dying aged thirty-five, but leaving behind an important work of crime fiction, full of inside information, *Clement Lorimer; or The Book with the Iron Clasps* (1849). Reach was for a time a friend of Vidocq, and from the stories obtained from the Frenchman, plus his own knowledge of the criminal underworld, wrote his strangely titled but engrossing book. Seven years later, another Scot, William Russell, writing under the name 'Waters' published *Recollections of a Detective Police-Officer*. Like Vidocq 'Waters' entered the police because of 'adverse circumstances chiefly the result of my own reckless follies', but soon caught the eye of his superior because of the 'ingenuity and boldness' he displayed, and went on to enjoy a most successful career.

Following the establishment of a proper police force by Sir Robert Peel in 1814, and its growth to a position of power and respect in the next few decades, it is not to be wondered that writers of the stature of Charles Dickens (1812–70) and Wilkie Collins (1824–89) should have seen in its activities material for their work. Dickens had actually been fascinated by police work since he was a youngster, and he knew a number of the Bow Street Runners. The criminal fraternity were not unknown to him, either, and he made several visits to Newgate Prison to talk to famous criminals of the day. Undoubtedly, though, his closest contact was with one of the leading policemen of the day, Inspector Field, whom he featured in a series of articles. One must also not forget Inspector Wicher, another famous name, who appears in *Three Detective Anecdotes* as 'Sergeant Witchem'. This same man, Witcher, was used by Dickens' friend, Wilkie Collins, as the model for Sergeant Cuff in his brilliant novel, *The Moonstone*, published in 1868. Collins appears to have formed his interest in crime while holidaying in Paris with Dickens — discovering in an old bookshop a copy of the *Newgate Calendar* from which, he later wrote, 'I found some of my best plots.' There are strong elements of mystery and detection in Collins' earlier work, *The Woman in White* (1860), which was enormously popular, but *The Moonstone* is his masterpiece, described by T. S. Eliot as 'the first, the longest and the best of all detective novels'.

(Facing page) The first full-length crime story was *Clement Lorimer; or, The Book with the Iron Clasps* by Angus Reach published in six monthly parts in 1848–49. The work was superbly illustrated by George Cruikshank who highlighted the racehorse doping, planting of evidence and kidnapping which were essential elements of the story. Reach, who had been a crime reporter at the Old Bailey and became friendly with the Frenchman Vidocq during his lecture tour of Britain, based his engrossing work on much real information.

Although Charles Dickens' *Barnaby Rudge* (1841) is primarily concerned with the Gordon anti-popery riots of 1780, there is a sub-plot dealing with the mysterious death of Mr Reuben Haredale, a country squire. Hablot K. Browne – who signed himself 'Phiz' – drew these engravings of Barnaby, who is wrongly accused of a crime and shut up in Newgate, and Mr Haredale defying the rioters. He excelled himself further with 'The Murderer Arrested' **(above)** and 'The Murderer's Confession' from a closing episode. Edgar Allan Poe was much intrigued with this serial while it was being published, and after a few episodes predicted the ending so accurately that even Dickens was amazed!

(Below) E. G. Dalziel drew this illustration for Dickens' 'Hunted Down', which first appeared in the *New York Ledger* in 1859. The story was based on the career of a poisoner, Thomas Wainewright, whom Dickens actually visited while in prison.

(Right) George Cruikshank's engraving of the Bow Street Runners, Blathers and Duff visiting Oliver in *Oliver Twist* (1838), in which Dickens first revealed his interest in crime and detection.

(Bottom) Inspector Bucket, the investigative officer who explains, in a dramatic dénouement, how he came to arrest the murderer in *Bleak House* (1853). Bucket, the first officer to be cast as a hero in fiction, is here searching Lady Deadlock's boudoir for clues to the case of blackmail and murder.

(Facing page) *The Mystery of Edwin Drood*, Dickens' detective story which he began early in 1870 but was unable to complete before his death in June of that year. The unfinished tale has presented crime-fiction readers over the years with one of their greatest mysteries — how did the author mean to resolve the case? Had the hero of the title been murdered, and what was the significance of the opium-smoking character, John Jasper? C. A. Collins drew the cover for the first issue, and Luke Fildes the engraving of Jasper in the opium den. The lower anonymous illustration is just one of many pictorial suggestions for an ending — the ghost of Edwin appearing to Jasper to reveal all!

(Opposite page) Wilkie Collins, a friend of Charles Dickens, also made a major contribution to crime fiction when he published *The Woman in White* as a serial beginning in 1859. This drawing by Frederick Walker caught the atmosphere and mystery of this 'most popular novel of its age'.

(Below left) Collins based his detective Sergeant Cuff in his other crime novel, *The Moonstone*, on a real figure, and the book is a masterpiece of invention, intricacies and counter-plot. These illustrations are from early English and American editions of the work.

(Below) Dalziel's illustration for 'The Stolen Letter', one of his short crime stories which was collected in *After Dark* (1856).

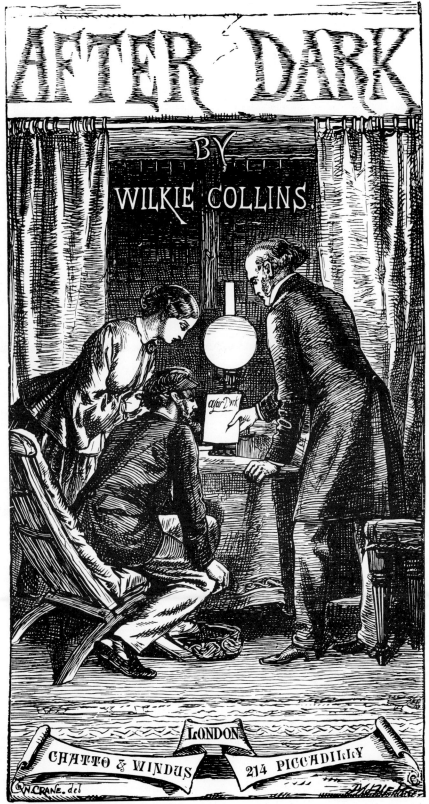

AFTER DARK

BY WILKIE COLLINS

LONDON

CHATTO & WINDUS

214 PICCADILLY

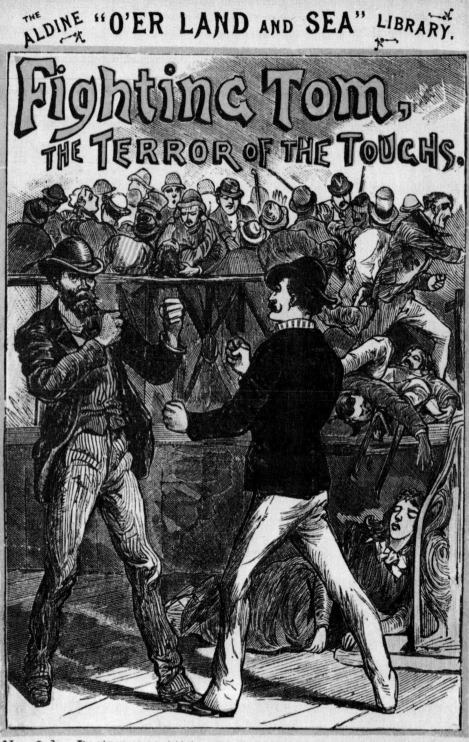

Fighting Tom,
THE TERROR OF THE TOUCHS.

No. 84]   The slim young man laid the woman gently down, and then faced the giant, quietly remarking, "Now, my friend, take care of yourself!"   [2d.

London: ALDINE PUBLISHING COMPANY.

Pictured above is 'Fighting' Thomas Harvey, a lawyer-detective who specialised in aiding the under-privileged of New York. The series was published by Aldine Publications on both sides of the Atlantic.

7. THE SENSATIONAL SLEUTHS

Twentieth-century detective fiction did not just spring on to the reading table; a generation of slim books with lurid cover illustrations was responsible for the popular notions about how detectives work and had thus provided the impetus.

J. RANDOLPH COX
Encyclopedia of Mystery and Detection

With the growing popularity of the detective story, it was not long before publishers began to widen the market for such works. In the main all fiction first appeared in two- and three-volume sets, and these were naturally expensive to purchase — so enterprising publishers began to produce cheap editions. These books became known as 'Railway Fiction', because they were gaudily packaged to catch the eye of the large numbers of train travellers, or more generally as 'Yellow Backs'. The books had colourful front covers with yellow spines — which gave them their name — and cost from sixpence to two shillings. Some stories appeared in even cheaper form with plain yellow covers — but the purpose of both was to convey light fiction to the masses.

By their very nature, books in this format were of a sensational kind, featuring law officers who were bold and extrovert. The stories of the Scottish author James M'Govan (1834–92) such as *Traced and Tracked, Brought to Bay, Hunted Down* and *Strange Clues*, which were all from the 'Casebook of a City Detective' named M'Sweeney, were typical of many more now long since confined to oblivion. M'Govan was hailed by *People's Friend*, as 'That genius M'Govan — surely the very *Dickens* of detectives!'

Popular though M'Govan and his other British contemporaries — like Major Arthur Griffiths and Mary Braddon — were, they could not match the success of Fergus Hume (1859–1932) whose novel *The Mystery of a Hansom Cab* was without doubt the best-selling novel of the nineteenth century and to be found in abundance wherever people travelled. Hume actually wrote and published the book himself in Australia in 1886, and when he came to England a few years later, foolishly sold the copyright for £50. Once re-published in 'Yellow Back' form it quickly sold over 350,000 copies — but the luckless Hume never saw another penny.

America, too, had its cheap publications in the form of the 'Dime Novels' which had originated from Irwin Beadle's publishing house in 1860. The majority of works in this format were originals rather than reprints, but they played a major part in introducing the detective story to American readers — and giving them several memorable characters. The early 'Dime Novels' tended to be intensely patriotic and featured Civil War and Wild West tales, though through these emerged one of the earliest frontier 'detectives', 'Deadwood Dick'. The first such publication entirely devoted to detectives was *Old Cap Collier Library* (1883–99) which specialised initially in reprinting translations of the Emile Gaboriau stories (an example appears in the section *Le Roman Policier*), and was followed almost immediately by *The New York Detective Library* (1883–98) with the stories of Old and Young King Brady. Other such publications followed in a flood, with perhaps the enduring Nick Carter as the most outstanding. Many of the American publishers, aware of the interest on the other side of the Atlantic, reprinted their best-selling series in Britain — and no one enjoyed better sales than the Aldine Company noted for its colourful and effective cover illustrations.

(Opposite page) Two of Fergus Hume's titles that began an era: *The Mystery of a Hansom Cab* (first published in Australia 1886) and *Madame Midas* (London, 1888). *Wyllard's Weird* by one of the most successful women writers of the period, Mary Braddon; and *Traced and Tracked* the Memoirs of a City Detective' by James McGovan (1884).
(Below) Perhaps the most famous of all 'railway novels', by Major Arthur Griffiths, with an illustration from a later edition (1896).

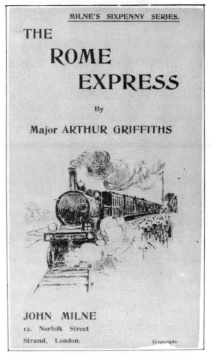

MILNE'S SIXPENNY SERIES.

THE
ROME
EXPRESS

By
Major ARTHUR GRIFFITHS

JOHN MILNE
12. Norfolk Street
Strand, London.

Allan Pinkerton, born the son of a
police sergeant in Scotland, but
moved to Chicago in 1842, was the
man who founded the now world-
famous Pinkerton Detective Agency.
After first serving as a deputy sheriff,
he opened the agency and then later
used the cases of his men as the basis
for a highly successful series of stories.
The publications always carried the
symbol of an eye and the motto, 'We
Never Sleep'. These three illustrations
are from the story 'The Molly Maguires
and the Detectives' (1877), about
Pinkerton's assignment to combat a
secret organisation engaged in indu-
strial unrest.

(Below) Cover of *Marianne The
Outcast*, one of the numerous cases
from 'The Diary of Detective Thorn'
and published in serial form on both
sides of the Atlantic at the turn of the
century.

(Facing page) Rare first issue of *Nick
Carter Detective Library* featuring the
master of disguise, published in 1891.
There were over a thousand more
issues like this until 1915, when Carter
— nicknamed 'The Little Giant' because
of his strength — changed format, and
he has continued to this day, though
he is now a paperback 'super agent'.
Only the English detective, Sexton
Blake, has undertaken more cases and
visited more locations than the evergreen Carter.

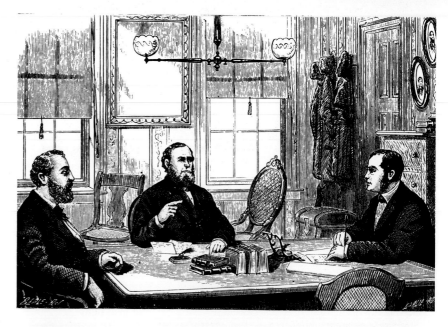

NICK CARTER

Nick Carter **IN VARIOUS** DISGUISES

DETECTIVE LIBRARY

The Only 5 Cent Detective Library Published.

Entered According to Act of Congress, in the Year 1891, by Street & Smith, in the Office of the Librarian of Congress, Washington, D. C.
Entered as Second-class Matter at the New York Post Office, N. Y., August 8, 1891.   Issued Weekly. Subscription Price, $2.50 per Year.

No. 1.   STREET & SMITH, Publishers,   **NEW YORK.**   31 Rose St., N. Y.   P. O. Box 2734.   5 Cents.

Nick Carter, Detective.
By A Celebrated Author.

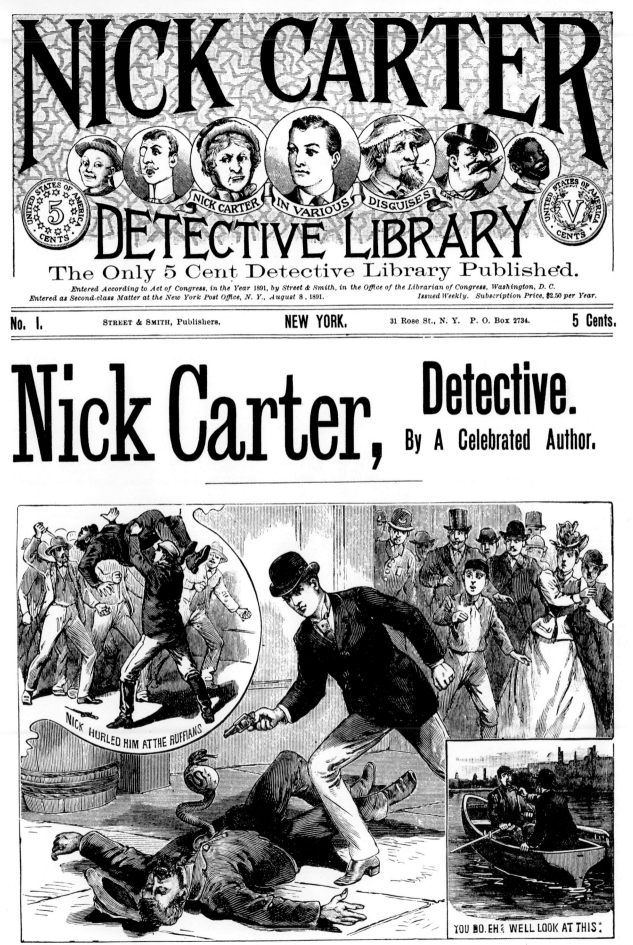

NICK HURLED HIM AT THE RUFFIANS

"YOU BO. EH? WELL LOOK AT THIS."

51

(Left) Three of the enormously popular Deadwood Dick adventures written by Edward L. Wheeler, beginning in 1877 and considered among the most important of American 'dime novels'. Although basically a frontiersman, Dick was a master at righting wrongs and detecting crime — and also at disguising himself. He had an occasional female compatriot named Kodak Kate. The series was continued long after Wheeler's death and spawned many imitators.

(Opposite) A colourful selection of some of the detective novels published in paper covers by the Aldine Publishing Company of London and New York. Many anonymous authors on both sides of the Atlantic contributed to the series.

(Below) Illustrations from two other Nick Carter tales: 'The Fate of Dr Quartz' — Dr Quartz was a mad-man Carter frequently encountered, who had a passion for dissecting beautiful girls (1891) — and at the bottom, 'Nick Carter's Mysterious Case' in which he was once again pitted against the syndicate of villains known as Daazar.

Old King Brady, who appeared in 1885, was perhaps the most believable of all the dime novel detectives, for he made mistakes, had no super-human powers and constantly found himself on the brink of disaster. Yet his creator, Francis Doughty, made him enormously popular through authentic detail and clever plotting. In later adventures, the New York detective was joined by Young King Brady who, surprisingly, was not a relative, and the two formed a most effective duo: almost certainly the first such in crime fiction. Chinese villains also made some of their earliest appearances in this series.

(Bottom) Three of the Aldine 'mini-size' crime novels which were noted for their tough themes.

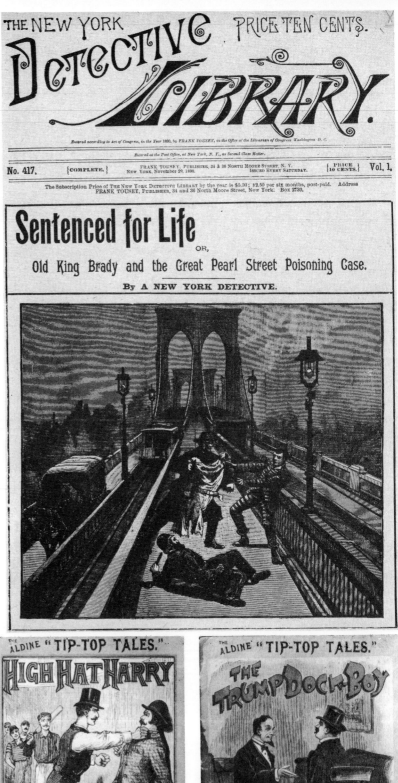

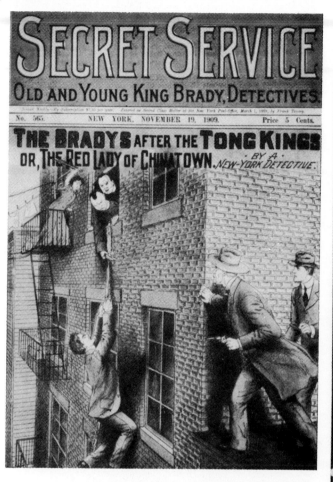

(Above) Frank Tousey was a New York publisher who specialised in detective tales, and his characters were just as likely to be found in cities as the Wild West. The infamous Frank and Jesse James were still alive when Tousey began featuring them in *Detective Library*, and it is true to say that no other characters have ever quite captured the public imagination as these two. D. W. Stevens, who recorded their adventures, invented virtually everything, and it was a mark of their popularity that they were often pitted against other 'dime novel' heroes and were never beaten.

(Left) England's most popular hero of this time was Jack Harkaway who, after running away from school, was involved in adventures all over the globe. The author of the series, Bracebridge Hemyng, a former barrister, liked elements of mystery and crime in his stories and Jack confronted many villains during his career, as in this incident from *Jack Harkaway's Schooldays* (1871). In 1874, Hemyng was lured to America where it was hoped he would repeat his success, but he never managed to duplicate the Harkaway popularity.

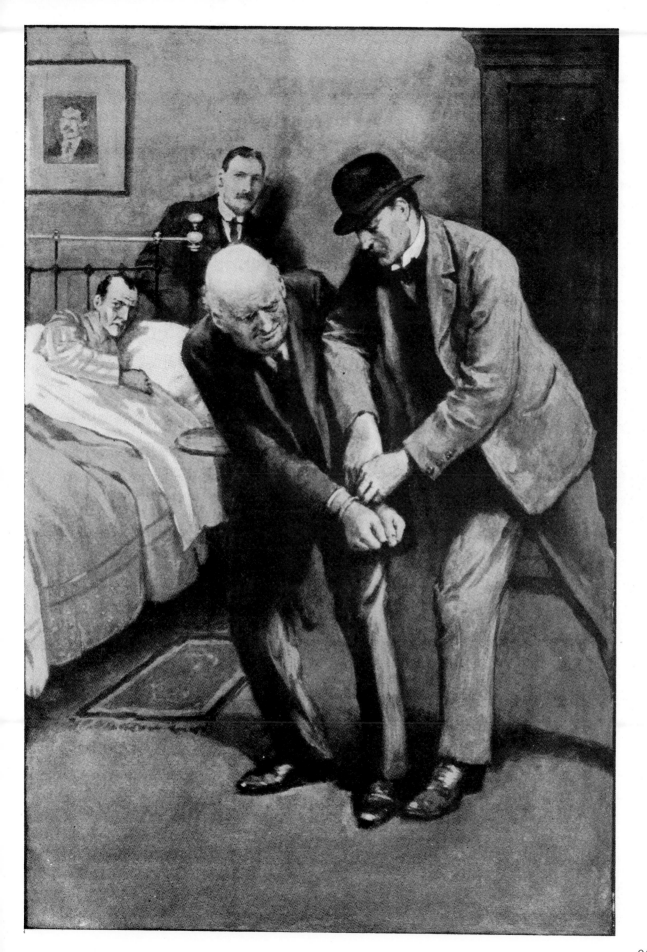

(Above and left) No publication is more closely identified with Sherlock Holmes than the *Strand*, and this cover, complete with miniature portrait, appeared in 1913, while the A. Gilbert picture was for 'His Last Bow' in September 1917.

(Bottom left) Two famous modern illustrators pick scenes only moments apart from 'The Speckled Band', for different magazine publications of the story appearing in the 1930s: John Mackay (left), and Ernest Wallcousins.

(Facing page) The international appeal of Holmes continues in many forms, and he is particularly popular in strip cartoons as these examples show. The 1950s picture versions by E. Meiser and Frank Giacoia have covered most of the Adventures and been widely reprinted around the world in English and translation. The cover of the *Marvel Comics* issue featuring 'The Hound of the Baskervilles' was by Ken Barr, 1976. The little vignette of Holmes and Watson peering round the chimney was for *The New Exploits of Sherlock Holmes* by Conan Doyle's son, Adrian, in partnership with John Dickson Carr, published in 1954. And Holmes' lighting his famous pipe was for the latest of the 'newly discovered' adventures, *The West End Horror* edited by Nicholas Meyer, 1976.

9. A RASH OF DETECTIVES

(Above) Although his work for crime and mystery stories was often the equal and frequently superior to that of Sidney Paget, Stanley L. Wood is scarcely remembered today. There can have been few more villainous-looking individuals than 'Slackjaw', a hunch-back criminal who features in Arthur Morrison's story of the unscrupulous private detective, Horace Dorrington, 'The Case of Mr Loftus Deacon', *Windsor Magazine*, 1897.

(Right) Two more illustrations from Morrison's tales of the cunning Dorrington;

(Top) A Sydney Cowell picture for 'The Case of the "Mirror of Portugal"' *Windsor*, 1896;

(Below) An excellent Stanley L. Wood painting of Dorrington intimidating a suspect in the curiously titled 'The Affair of the "Avalance Bicycle and Tyre Co. Ltd"', *Windsor*, 1896.

(Previous page) Sir Arthur Conan Doyle was responsible for completing his friend Grant Allen's story 'Hilda Wade' when the novelist fell fatally ill in 1899. Sir Arthur penned 'The Episode of the Dead Man Who Spoke', which was superbly illustrated for publication the following year by Gordon Browne.

Although the interest in detective fiction was increasing all the time, it was the appearance of the Sherlock Holmes novels which gave the genre the biggest impetus in its history. Suddenly the bookshops and railway station stalls were full of rival detectives in the Holmes tradition and arch villains who might make even the redoubtable Professor Moriarty or Colonel Moran seem somewhat tame. These two groups we shall be studying in specific sections later: here we shall look just at the writers who followed immediately in Sir Arthur Conan Doyle's footsteps.

Arthur Morrison (1863–1945) who actually prided himself more on his books about the appalling social conditions of the time, such as *Tales of Mean Streets* (1894), was the next writer to make his mark on the genre, and it has to be said that his detective, Martin Hewitt, not only practised the same methods as Holmes, but shared the same magazine and illustrator, the *Strand* and Sidney Paget! Perhaps more original is his sometime conman and private detective, Horace Dorrington. Almost as quickly on the scene was journalist Robert Barr (1850–1912), another Scot, who is best remembered as the founder with Jerome K. Jerome of the popular humour magazine, *The Idler*. He also scored two 'firsts' with the earliest parody of the Holmes cases, *Detective Stories Gone Wrong*, and created Eugene Valmont, the first humorous detective of any standing, and a forerunner of Hercule Poirot.

A friend of Sir Arthur Conan Doyle's, Grant Allen (1848–99), author of the sensational sex novel *The Woman Who Did* (1895), which caused a scandal in Victorian England, not surprisingly made his own contributions to the genre in the early years of the boom. So, too, did the Australian, Guy Boothby (1867–1905), who came to England and made such an impact that his friend Rudyard Kipling wrote, 'Mr Guy Boothby has come to great honours now. His name is large upon the hoardings, his books sell like hot cakes.'

While the British were very much leading the way in the genre at this moment in time, the French still managed to weigh in with a very important contribution by Gaston Leroux (1868–1927), a former crime reporter and war correspondent who wrote one of the most famous thrillers of all time, the much-filmed *Phantom of the Opera* (1911). What he contributed to detective fiction, though, was *The Mystery of the Yellow Room* (1907), one of the first stories in which the murderer turns out to be the least suspected person in the story! Of Leroux's equally famous compatriot, Maurice Leblanc, we shall hear more later.

It is, of course, no surprise to find that a number of the leading writers of the period, such as Robert Louis Stevenson, Israel Zangwill, Rider Haggard and even Arnold Bennett, dabbled in the genre and produced works which, while they may not be among their very best, still remain important to all students of literature. In truth, this was a time when crime and mystery fiction showed all the signs of an epidemic among authors and readers alike.

Kidnappers pounce on the rich man 'whose fortune had been accumulated by speculation in Australia' in an early detective story by George R. Sims, 'Dramas of Life' illustrated by J. H. Russell (1890).

(Top) Robert Barr was another early success in the 'Detective Boom' and his series 'Tales of Revenge' proved very popular in *The English Illustrated Magazine*. The distinguished artist

Lancelot Speed drew these two pictures for 'A Dynamite Explosion', March 1894. Barr was also responsible under a pseudonym for one of the first Holmes parodies, 'Detective Stories Gone Wrong' in *The Idler*, with illustrations by George Hutchinson

(1892). Here 'Sherlaw Kombs' is shown relaxing — and on the trail of criminals, with his assistant, 'Dr Whatson', actually doing the dirty work.

Major Arthur Griffiths was also to the fore at this time, and featured a nobleman detective, Sir Isaac Falconer, in 'Locked Up', illustrated by C. J. Staniland in 1887.
(Above) Sir Arthur is captured by a criminal in disguise and his gang, and **(below right)** the criminal, Patch, who is at the centre of the mystery.
(Below) An early Scotland Yard hero, Inspector Heron, here in disguise, with his assistant, on the trail of a villain in 'The Duke Decides' by Headon Hill (1903).

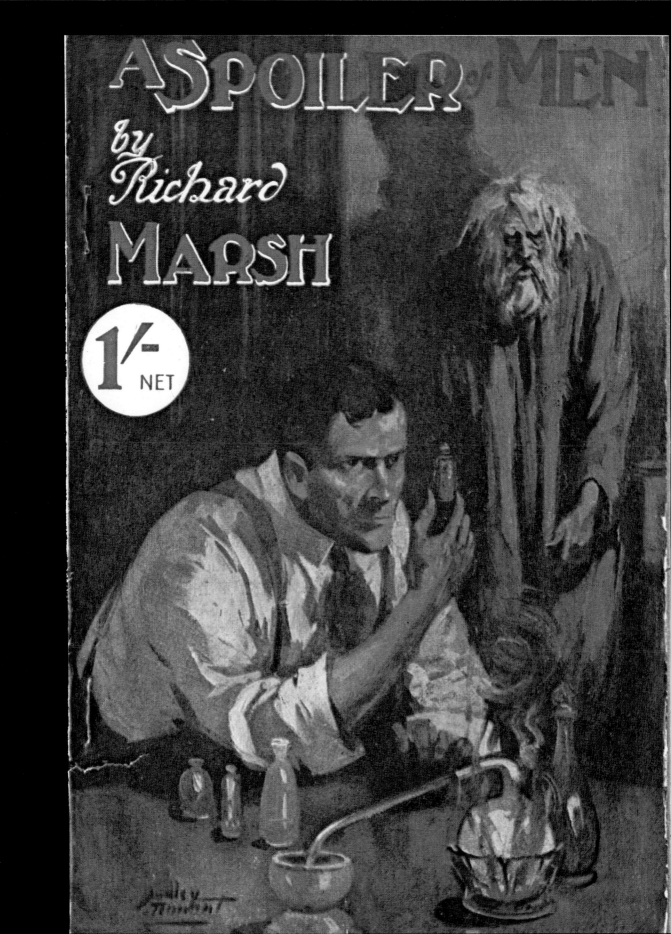

A SPOILER of MEN

by Richard MARSH

1/-
NET

(Facing page) Coloured front cover by Dudley Tennant for much sought-after novel by Richard Marsh, a rather underrated early master of the mystery and detective novel (1905).

(Top) Frontispiece from Richard Marsh's most famous story 'The Beetle', a crime and horror tale still eminently readable today. This illustration was by John Williamson (1897). **(Top right and above)** Two of the popular Dick Donovan mystery tales: Calvin Sugg, detective, in a dramatic moment drawn by Gordon Browne for 'Tracked to Doom' (1892); and a Fred Barnard illustration for 'The Dead Man's Secret' (1889).

Few crime and mystery stories were more popular at the turn of the century, yet more completely forgotten today, than those of the Australian Guy Boothby who wrote over fifty novels and died aged only thirty-eight. Dr Nikola, his famous villain, is illustrated later, but here are three typical examples of his work: **(Top)** 'The Woman of Death' drawn by Victor Prout, 1900, and 'The Red Rat's Daughter', by Henry Austin, 1899; and **(left)** Stanley L. Wood's illustration for 'The Kidnapped President', 1902.

(Facing page, top left) 'The Crime Doctor', one of the first detectives to solve crimes by psychology, was a creation of E. W. Hornung of 'Raffles' fame, here illustrated by Frederic Dorr Steele, 1914.

(Top right) R. Austin Freeman, who created the famous Dr Thorndyke, wrote some earlier detective tales, 'The Adventures of Romney Pringle' in 1902, under the pseudonym of Clifford Ashdown, which are now very rare collectors' items.

The skilled Gaston Leroux, who was the French master of mystery at this time, wrote a classic of detection, *The Mystery of the Yellow Room* in 1907, which introduced a precocious young reporter-cum-detective, Rouletabille, who explains a virtually insoluble case of a murder in a locked room – one of the first mysteries of this kind.

Israel Zangwill, the novelist and social activist, has been hailed as 'The Father of the Locked-Room Mystery' for his book, *The Big Bow Mystery* published in 1892. Another ingenious mystery from his pen was 'Cheating the Gallows' (*The Idler*, 1893) in which a man cleverly builds up two very different identities – one of which commits a murder and 'disappears'. George Hutchinson drew these pictures.

(Below) Turn-of-the-century 'Black Maria' – a picture by Frank Feller, also from *The Idler*, 1895.

The informer has always been a powerful ally of the detective and the policeman, as these three examples demonstrate.

(Top left) One of the earliest illustrations of an informer, 'The Queer Old Man', who appears in B. L. Farjeon's *Blade O' Grass* 1874

(Above) A tip-off from a priest helps Paul Beck, 'The Rule of Thumb Detective', in the story of the same name by Irish barrister-novelist, M. McDonnell Bodkin, published in 1898. Bodkin also created 'Dora Myrl, the Lady Detective' who, after adventures of her own, eventually married Beck, and they had a son who took up crime solving as well!

(Left) A scrap of information imparted in a casino proves a vital clue for Edmund Martin in E. Phillips Oppenheim's story 'The Tortoiseshell Princess' illustrated by Cyrus Cuneo in the *Premier Magazine*, 1915. Oppenheim, who was known as 'the Prince of Storytellers', set most of his 150 books in wealthy society, being well in tune with this world through his own enormous literary earnings and glamorous life in the South of France.

Murder on the railway was a popular theme with several early detective story writers, and Eden Phillpotts' novel, *My Adventure in the Flying Scotsman* (1888), is both one of the earliest on the theme and most famous **(above)**. Phillpotts, who is better known for his rural novels, did write several mysteries under the pen-name of Harrington Hext, and he played an important part in encouraging Agatha Christie to take up crime writing.
(Top left) Another famous writer who dabbled in mysteries was Sir Arthur Quiller Couch. This picture illustrates his 'The Troop Train Murder' in the *Premier Magazine*, July 1915, in which he constructed a mystery story and then turned it over to Baroness Orczy, who used her famous detective, Lady Molly, to solve it successfully. Perhaps the best of the railway mystery writers was Canon Victor Whitechurch, a scholarly English churchman who devised some tough and ingenious plots, usually featuring railway detective Thorpe Hazell.
(Left) Alfred Paget picture for Whitechurch's 'A Station Master's Story', *Strand*, 1899.
(Right) The Canon's 'Saved by a Train Wrecker' illustrated by W. D. Almond, *Strand*, 1899, and **(far right)** Thorpe Hazell in a deadly situation in Gordon Browne's sketch for 'The Convict's Revenge' *Strand*, 1898.

Four more distinguished Victorian novelists who wrote successful crime stories.

(Above) Clues to a mystery were written on a young woman's back in Rider Haggard's 'Mr Meeson's Will', 1904. Humorist Jerome K. Jerome's rare crime tale 'The Street of the Blank Wall' in *The Premier*, May 1916.

(Far left) Robert Louis Stevenson wrote several mysteries, including *The Wrong Box* in partnership with Lloyd Osbourne, 1893.

(Left) Modern design for Arnold Bennett's volume of short detective tales featuring Cecil Thorold, a wealthy and highly unorthodox sleuth. These stories were all written by Bennett in a two-month period in 1903.

(Facing page)
William Le Queux, mystery writer and allegedly former British Secret Service Agent, wrote numerous stories predicting intrigues and even conflicts between nations which proved uncannily accurate.

(Far right) Documents reproduced in his book which forecast the First World War, *The Invasion of 1910*, published in 1905.

(Right) Russian setting for Le Queux's *Secret Service* (1896) – a country which banned several of his books.

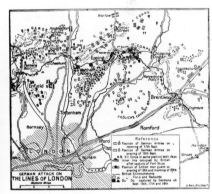

10. THE RIVALS OF SHERLOCK HOLMES

The amiable yet cleverly analytical Martin Hewitt was the first popular detective to follow in the footsteps of Sherlock Holmes — even to the extent of appearing in the *Strand* magazine. The creation of Arthur Morrison, a journalistic social commentator and art expert, Hewitt's adventures are chron-chronicled by a reporter named Brett. **(Above left)** Sidney Paget drew the illustrations for *The Case of the Dixon Torpedo*; and **(right)** this representation of Hewitt and Brett about to seek evidence underwater in *The Nicobar Bullion Case*.
(Left) The two men looking for clues among the dead in *The Quinton Jewel Affair* (1894).

(Previous page) Max Pemberton's unusual detective Bernard Sutton who dealt in crimes concerned with precious stones, caught in the act of listening to two criminals — a sketch by R. Caton Woodville for the *English Illustrated Magazine's* publication of 'Jewel Mysteries I Have Known' in 1893.

The rivals of Sherlock Holmes have remained for too long in the shadow of the master. Some were honest men: some were crooks: all were formidable. From Holborn and the Temple in the east, to Richmond in the west, they dominated the criminal underworld of late Victorian and Edwardian London, sometimes rescuing their clients, sometimes eliminating them.

HUGH GREENE
The Rivals of Sherlock Holmes

As was indicated in the previous section, once Sherlock Holmes had made his appearance on the detective scene, rivals of all kinds sprang from the pens of contemporary writers and went about their many and varied cases in great numbers until the advent of World War I. The magazines of the time like the *Strand, Windsor, Pearson's* and *Harmsworth's* played an important role in fostering these sleuths, and those that found favour with readers were soon accorded the permanence of hard cover publication. Today both the original magazines and books are highly prized collectors' items, and the illustrations which appeared in them — as this section will demonstrate — are both dramatic and evocative of a period of gas-lit streets, hansom cabs and evil deeds in the shadows.

Although Martin Hewitt, Arthur Morrison's detective, was the first detective to become widely popular after Holmes, the hardworking journalist, Dick Donovan (1843–1934), was actually into print first with his series, *The Man Hunter: Stories from the Note Book of a Detective* in 1888, the first of several series of tales in which the author featured himself as a detective, although his knowledge was all second-hand! Hard on his heels came Max Pemberton (1863–1950), another busy contributor to magazines of the period and himself the editor of *Cassell's* magazine. Though scarcely read today, his tales of Bernard Sutton who investigates jewellery crimes are both exciting and original.

The era also saw the appearance of one of the greatest of all scientific detectives, Dr John Thorndyke, created by R. Austin Freeman (1862–1943). Thorndyke has the rare distinction of being the only literary criminologist whose fictional methods were actually put into use by the real police. Howard Haycraft has left us in no doubt as to his importance: 'He was the true and undoubted "parent" of the scientific detective story in the highest meaning of the phrase, and remains today the dean of that form — if not, indeed, of all detective story writers of whatever style or persuasion.' The year 1909 saw the arrival of the first of the 'armchair detectives', Baroness Orczy's 'Old Man in the Corner' who solves cases while sitting in the corner of a tea shop twiddling a piece of string. The Hungarian-born Baroness (1865–1947) also created the first of a long line of shady lawyers in Patrick Mulligan, whose methods on behalf of his clients are not above transgressing the law.

These are just some of Holmes' rivals to be found in the following pages — there are more 'stars', such as the remarkable blind detective, Max Carrados, written by Ernest Bramah (1868–1942); the great G. K. Chesterton's (1874–1936) delightful Father Brown; and that unique figure November Joe from the Canadian backwoods, created by Hesketh Pritchard (1876–1922). All of them gave 'The Great Detective' a run for his popularity in the magazines and books of the day.

'Paul Campenhaye: Specialist in Criminology' in a dangerous situation pictured by Paul Durden for the story 'The Magician of Cannon Street' (1918). Campenhaye was written by Joseph S. Fletcher, a prolific English novelist, who suddenly found international acclaim after his book, *The Middle Temple Murder* (1918), was highly praised by American President Woodrow Wilson.

A ROMANCE FROM A DETECTIVE'S CASE·BOOK

Dick Donovan was the pseudonym of a widely travelled London special correspondent, Joyce Emmerson Muddock, who utilised his knowledge to great effect in his dozens of mystery and detective books, the popularity of which he deplored. Donovan featured himself as a strong and resourceful crime fighter in his popular series for the *Strand* magazine, 'Romances From A Detective's Casebook' (1892), with drawings by Paul Hardy.

(Above left) 'The Secret of the Black Brotherhood' and **(right)** 'The Chamber of Shadows'. At right, Donovan examines a trunk in 'The Story of the Great Cat's Eye'.

More illustrations by R. Caton Woodville from Max Pemberton's 'Jewel Mysteries I Have Known' mentioned at the start of this section. **(Top)** Bernard Sutton confronted by the mystery of *The Necklace of Green Diamonds* and **(above left)** seen as a man for the ladies in *Treasure of White Creek* — but note the ominous hand coming round the door!

(Above right) Sutton discovers the victim of ruthless men after *The Seven Emeralds*, and **(far right)** the jewel sleuth makes a successful arrest in the case of *The Ripening Rubies* — a sketch this time by Fred Barnard. Author Max Pemberton, who spent many years as an editor and newspaper executive, was knighted in 1928.

Major Arthur Griffiths, a popular writer during the early years of the detective story genre, never quite repeated the success of his much reprinted *The Rome Express* (1896). He did, though, make good use of his military service in many far-flung locations, when writing his series, 'In Tight Places: Adventures of an Amateur Detective', for *The English Illustrated Magazine*, 1897–98. The hero, Lionel Macnaughton-Innes, investigated crime at sea in 'A Spanish Mine' **(top right)** and in Egypt in 'Yussuf the Dragonman' **(top left).** Indeed he ranged throughout the Far East in 'Queen Hatasoo's Pectoral' and there were plans to bring him to Europe, but sadly the magazine folded and these never materialised.

(Facing page) Superb colour portrait of Guy Boothby's sinister Dr Nikola by Stanley L. Wood (1896).

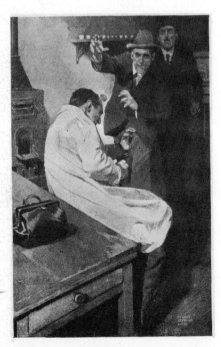

Dr John Thorndyke has rightly been described as the greatest medico-legal detective of all time, and his cases written by R. Austin Freeman are masterpieces of examination and analysis. Dr Thorndyke is a tall, handsome man, with a superb mind, who is supported in his enquiries by an aide, Jervis, and a brilliant laboratory assistant, Nathaniel Polton. Like Conan Doyle, Austin Freeman trained as a medical man, but ill-health brought on while practising in Africa forced him to give up this work and he returned to England and took up writing. His later contributions to the detective and mystery genre place him in many people's eyes on the same level as Conan Doyle. Dr Thorndyke remains his classic contribution, and the illustrations on this page are **(above)** by Reginald Cleaver for 'The Magic Casket', *Pearson's*, October 1926, and **(left)** by Sydney Seymour Lucas for 'The New Jersey Sphinx', also *Pearson's*, April 1922.

R. Austin Freeman was fond of including explanatory diagrams or photographs of actual clues in his Dr Thorndyke stories.
(Facing page) Howard E. Elcock's picture for 'The Apparition of Burling Court' and a diagram "The mystery of the inverted head explained" from *Pearson's*, March 1923.
(Right) Dr Thorndyke with his aide and chronicler, Christopher Jervis, drawn by H. M. Brock, and **(far right)** another Brock drawing for 'The Stranger's Latchkey', *Pearson's*, January 1909.

The mystery of the inverted head explained.

Two illustrations by Warwick Reynolds, another superb Victorian magazine illustrator now scarcely remembered, for R. Austin Freeman's series, 'A Hunter of Criminals' in *Pearson's*, 1913. In these tales, Professor Humphrey Challoner, whose wife has been killed by an unknown burglar, devotes his life to luring such criminals to his house, killing them, and then forming a collection of their skeletons and shrunken heads!

(Opposite page) The first of the 'armchair detectives' – the nameless old man who sits in a London tea shop solving the most baffling cases simply by analysing all the clues which are brought to him by a young female reporter, Polly Burton. The creation of Baroness Orczy of 'Scarlet Pimpernel' fame, 'The Old Man in the Corner' shows himself to be sympathetic towards the criminals and there is more than a hint in his last case, 'The Mysterious Death in Percy Street', that he may even have been a master criminal himself! The stories of the old man, knotting and unknotting a piece of string while he deduces, first appeared in *The Royal Magazine*, 1901–2, with illustrations by H. M. Brock. **(Top left)** The Old Man and Polly Burton. **(Top right)** 'The Regent's Park Murder'. **(Right)** 'The Percy Street Murder' and **(far right)** 'The Mysterious Death on the Underground Railway'.

Another 'first' achieved by Baroness Orczy was the creation of Patrick Mulligan, nick-named 'Skin O' My Tooth', the earliest unscrupulous English lawyer who will go to virtually any length to solve crimes. His portrait **(left),** and a scene in which he appears in disguise are by Gilbert Oakdale for 'The Clue of the Inverted Five' from *Pearson's,* August 1927.

(Below left) Another medical sleuth, 'Cinders' created by William Le Queux for *The Premier Magazine,* 1916, was a master of make-up, as was Archibald P. Batts, the millionaire detective hero of Emeric Hulme-Beaman's series in *The English Illustrated Magazine* in 1900. Malcolm Patterson drew this picture of Batts confronting his amazed chronicler, Mr Bertram, in 'The Adventure of the Italian Organ-Grinder'.

(Facing page) The remarkable blind detective, Max Carrados, the first of his kind in the genre, is a wealthy man, blinded in his youth, who has developed his senses and facilities to such a degree that he can devote his life to crime solving. He has an assistant, Parkinson, who serves as his 'eyes', and a disbarred solicitor who has become a private investigator. This remarkable group were created by Ernest Bramah, an extremely reticent English author, who for a time in his life was believed to be merely the pen-name of a famous writer! These three illustrations of Carrados in tight corners are all by the talented Warwick Reynolds for 'The Missing Witness Sensation', *Pearson's,* July 1926.

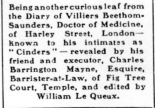

Being another curious leaf from the Diary of Villiers Beethom-Saunders, Doctor of Medicine, of Harley Street, London—known to his intimates as "Cinders"—revealed by his friend and executor, Charles Barrington Mayne, Esquire, Barrister-at-Law, of Fig Tree Court, Temple, and edited by William Le Queux.

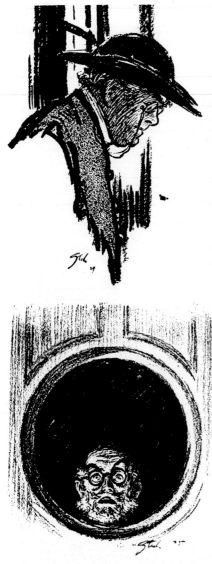

Regarded as one of the three most famous detectives in literature (Holmes and Dupin are the others), Father Brown is a gentle and courteous Roman Catholic priest who solves crimes almost effortlessly, but always hopes that the criminals will repent rather than have to be punished! G. K. Chesterton, his creator was a prolific writer and larger-than-life London personality, much of whose work remains in print to this day. The illustrations here are all from the American *Harper's Monthly Magazine* and drawn by the famous Frederic Dorr Steele.

(Top left) A portrait of Father Brown from 'The Mirror of Death', March 1925, and beside it the little priest keeping an eye on a murder suspect in the same story.

(Above) The central figure of the story 'The Man With Two Beards' April 1925, and **(right)** Father Brown interrogating a group of people involved in this bizarre case.

(Above) G. K. Chesterton was himself a skilled artist as this sketch which he drew for his first mystery book, *The Club of Queer Trades*, demonstrates (1905).

(Right) Horne Fisher, Chesterton's other zealous gentleman detective, who has become known as 'The Man Who Knew Too Much'.
This second of his cases related by journalist Harold March, 'The Vanishing Prince', was illustrated by W. Hatherell in *Harper's*, August 1920.

(Below) Two more outstanding Dorr Steele pictures for the Father Brown story, 'The Chief Mourner of Marne' which dealt with the last duel fought in England, *Harper's*, May 1925.

Perhaps the most curious and original of detectives is November Joe, a young Canadian woodsman cast in the tradition of the Red Indians whom experts see as the original detectives because of their skill in deducing evidence from the smallest clues. November Joe was created by Hesketh Pritchard, a redoubtably English novelist, traveller and military hero, who lived a most active life despite a heart defect. W. R. Stott drew the pictures for Joe's adventures in *Pearson's* magazine in 1912: **(Far left)** 'The Mystery of the Black Fox Skin' and 'The Case of Miss Virginia Planx'; and **(above)** 'The Crime at Big Tree Portage'. **(Left)** Those indomitable guardians of the law, the Canadian Mounties, also featured in several novels and stories, such as these two examples, both drawn by S. Tresilian for *Pearson's*: 'The Debt' by Sewell Peaslee Wright (1930), and 'Thirst' by C. V. Tench (1931).

II. THE AMERICAN CRIME FIGHTERS

(**Previous page**) 'Look out,' cried the detective, 'or you will get yourself into trouble', G. Hyde's illustration for *Hand and Ring*, an 1883 crime novel by Anna K. Greene, the American 'Mother of the Detective Story'. On this page are pictures for three more of the works by this remarkable woman, including **(top)** an anonymous illustration for *The Leavenworth Case* published in 1878 and generally agreed to be the first detective novel written by a woman.

(**Below**) The sinister *Doctor Izard* pictured by George Willis Bardwell, 1895, and **(right)** Adolf Thiede's painting of the search for hidden bank notes in *Agatha Webb* written in 1900.

This sound and objective view of the American detective story seems to underline the assertion by more than one writer that Poe gave the genre such a spectacular send-off that it was virtually impossible for any fellow countryman to match him for years to come. But this is not to say that America did not have some notable writers who made important contributions; rather that in the ensuing years they have become overshadowed in the genre.

Though the fact is not mentioned as often as it might be, America can claim 'The Mother of the Detective Story' as well as Poe, its sire. The lady was Mrs Anna Rohlfs (1846–1935), who as Anna Katharine Greene published the first detective novel by a woman, *The Leavenworth Case*, in 1878. This rather shy and unprepossessing woman was the daughter of a well-known New York lawyer and it has been suggested that this family background was the impetus for her writing tales of crime and mystery. In any event, *The Leavenworth Case* is remarkable in its skilled unfolding of a crime and the patient detective work of the investigator, Mr Ebenezer Gryce. The success of the book was immediate and Anna Greene was launched on a highly successful career which brought forth nearly forty more titles.

Credit for launching the first great American fictional detective goes to Melville Davisson Post (1869–1930), who reached back into the pre-Civil War decades of his country to create Uncle Abner, a strongly religious Virginian who sees himself as ordained by God to solve crime and administer justice in a neck of the woods where no organised law force exists. Post himself was first a lawyer, then became a highly successful magazine writer, declared by several critics to be the best American short story writer since Edgar Allan Poe. Apart from Uncle Abner, Post also created Randolph Mason, a crooked lawyer bent on saving his clients from justice by any means – his name was later carried on by that pillar of legal justice, Perry Mason!

(Top) Uncle Abner, 'the warlord in the army of God' who battles against the forces of evil and is claimed to be the first truly great American detective. Author Melville Davisson Post was first a lawyer and then writer creating numerous memorable detective characters but none quite the equal of Uncle Abner, here drawn by Enid Schantz.
Dramatic illustration by Dudley Hardy for Gilbert Burgess's story 'The Confession of Claude Leigh', an early detective short story in *The Century* magazine, September 1894.

The great Mark Twain (1835–1910) was deeply interested in the crime story, and is credited with having first utilised fingerprints as a method of detecting a criminal in *The Tragedy of Pudd'nhead Wilson* (1894). Apart from his other works with serious crime elements, he also exposed confidence tricksters in *The Celebrated Jumping Frog of Calaveras County* (1867), and satirised the whole genre in *Simon Wheeler, Detective* which was left unfinished at the time of his death. Another first for American detective fiction was the use of a lie detector in *The Man Higher Up* story by the partnership of Edwin Balmer (1883–1959) and William MacHarg (1872–1951), who created the first psychological detective, Luther Trant, in 1910. Arthur B. Reeve (1880–1936) also created a scientific sleuth in Craig Kennedy, who became the most popular detective in America in the 1910s and the first to become widely appreciated in Britain. The Craig Kennedy stories were in fact to bridge the gap between the old style of American crime story and the emergence in the 1920s of the 'Hardboiled' detectives in the pulp magazines.

The immortal Mark Twain made a significant contribution to the detective story, and was the first writer to use the method of fingerprinting as a means of identification. He first developed the idea in a short story in 1883, but put it to full use in *The Tragedy of Pudd'nhead Wilson* (1894) in which Pudd'nhead explains a crime by demonstrating how everyone's prints are quite different. Louis Loeb drew the two pictures at the top of the page for this book, the first showing Pudd'nhead in a tricky situation and the other him explaining how finger-prints on a windowsill may be 'read'. Twain wrote several other detective stories including the famous 'Tom Sawyer, Detective' and 'A Double-barrelled Detective Story' **(right)** which parodied the Sherlock Holmes' stories in recounting the adventures in the Wild West of Holmes' 'uncle', Fetlock Jones (1902).

The Inmate of the Dungeon.

By W C Morrow.

(Left) An early short story about crime and detection in prison by W. C. Morrow, an inventive writer of mystery and crime stories who is now enjoying something of a revival after years of neglect. 'The Inmate of the Dungeon', with its dramatic revelation of a crime by presenting the murder weapon to a prisoner, was illustrated by W. Cubitt Cooke for *Harper's*, January 1898.

(Above) The eccentric Professor Augustus S. F. X. Van Dusen, whose amazing logical ability has caused him to be nick-named 'The Thinking Machine', can solve cases of the utmost complexity. Jacques Futrelle, the creator of this bizarre figure, was a journalist for much of his life and is remembered for his heroic death during the sinking of the *Titanic*. 'The Thinking Machine' has his cases brought to him at the Boston College where he works by reporter Hutchinson Hatch, and the most engrossing of these is surely 'The Problem of Cell 13' in which he escapes from a prison cell for a bet.

(Left) Frank R. Stockton, the author of numerous juvenile stories and popular novels, also wrote several crime and mystery stories including the classic, 'The Lady, or The Tiger?' in which the reader must decide the solution. The anonymous illustration here was for his dramatic tale, 'The Snowflake of the Service', *The Century*, 1899.

(Left) Four illustrations by the excellent Stanley L. Wood for Dr Rodriguez Ottolengui's 1894 series of adventures about the crime-solving partnership of Mr Barnes, the professional detective, and Mr Mitchel, the wealthy amateur.
(Top left) Mr Barnes drops a coin to one of his informers in 'The Montezuma Emerald', and then watches a New York policeman arrest a kidnapper in 'A Singular Abduction' In the lower pictures Barnes and Mitchel seize a murderer whom Mr Barnes has been trailing through the city — both pictures from 'The Montezuma Emerald'.
Dr Ottolengui, incidentally, was a famous American dentist, and the author of a classic work, *Methods of Filling Teeth!*
(Right) Map of the district served by the lawyer-detective, Quincy Adams Sawyer, created by Charles Felton Pidgin. C. W. Reed illustrated the cases of the quiet and gentle lawyer who none the less handles himself well when in a tight corner.
(Below) 'The Man of Forty Faces', Hamilton Cleek, whose peculiar facial skin enables him to transform himself into many different characters without the need of make-up. His creator, Thomas Hanshew, also transformed him from his earliest adventures, when he was an international criminal, into an officer of the law feared on both sides of the Atlantic. Here he is making an arrest of a notorious *femme fatale* in *Cleek of Scotland Yard* (1912).

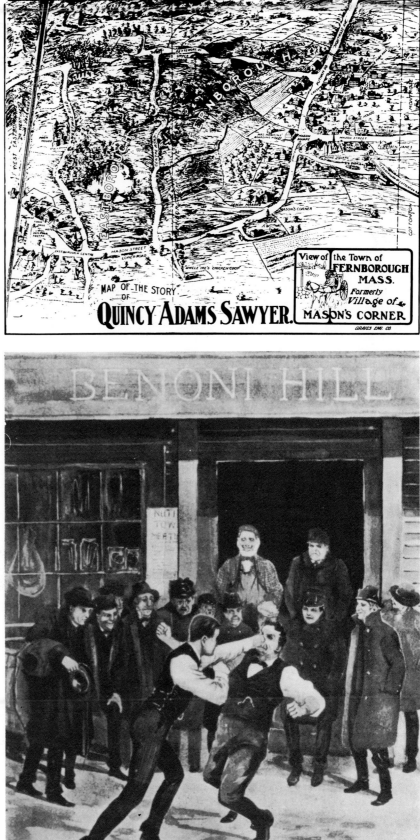

Described at the height of his fame as the 'American Sherlock Holmes', Craig Kennedy, a Professor at Columbia University, appeared in millions of books and magazines in the early years of this century. His author, Arthur B. Reeve, predicted many advances in criminology in the stories, and Kennedy was certainly one of the first truly scientific detectives. His popularity was also attributed to the fact that a young girl named Elaine appeared in many of the stories and always had to be rescued from the most dire situations by the resourceful Kennedy. **(Left)** 1920s illustration for the Kennedy case of 'The Exploits of Elaine' and **(above)** Margaret Brundage. *Weird Tales'* famous artist, did this cover for 'The Death Cry'. May 1935. Amos Sewell, another pulp specialist, was the artist for *Thrilling Detective's.* August 1934 issue which pitted Kennedy against some fiendish orientals

Apart from being the most successful American reporter of his time, Richard Harding Davis was a skilful writer of mystery stories, such as the short but very effective 'In The Fog', 1902, which Frederic Dorr Steele illustrated **(right)**.
Another short story, 'Playing Dead' **(below)** published in *The Century*, May 1916, appeared just before his death and was illustrated by Watson Charlton.
(Far right) Describing himself as 'the best detective in New York', 'Fatty' Welch (alias Wilkins) is a man of many parts and disguises who appeared in a series of stories written by the lawyer-author, Arthur Train. Wilkins was one of several characters created by Train, who also had the distinction of having authored some of the first books about true crime in America. This picture for 'The Escape of Wilkins' was by F. C. Yohn for *Scribner's*, July 1905.

Shagbark Jones, charlatan and quack, was described by his first publishers as 'quite the most original detective that ever stepped'. The humorous stories of this old faker were written by Ellis Parker Butler, author of the famous story 'Pigs Is Pigs', and creator of the inept Philo Gubb, Correspondence School Detective. Shagbark Jones operated with a mixture of cunning and logic and not a small helping of the supernatural.

(Above) Nathan Dean illustrates Jones' powers for 'The Mortgage Money', *Scribner's*, 1918; and **(right)** communing with the dead in 'The Mystery Man', 1918.

(Far right) A Shagbark Jones potion put to good, though not necessarily lawful, purpose in *The Mystery That Wasn't*, 1918.

(Above and below) A. C. Dann illustrations for *The Coral of Idris* by H. Bedford Jones, a prolific author of the period who wrote crime, mystery and fantasy stories, usually in exotic locations.

(Right) American diplomat Richard Washburn Child wrote a number of notable mystery stories including 'The Bomb' for which W. E. Wightman provided this picture, *Scribner's*, 1921.

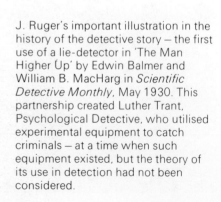

J. Ruger's important illustration in the history of the detective story — the first use of a lie-detector in 'The Man Higher Up' by Edwin Balmer and William B. MacHarg in *Scientific Detective Monthly*, May 1930. This partnership created Luther Trant, Psychological Detective, who utilised experimental equipment to catch criminals — at a time when such equipment existed, but the theory of its use in detection had not been considered.

A blind man who utilises the 'eyes' of science to solve a crime featured in MacHarg and Balmer's other out-standing collaboration, *The Blind Man's Eyes*, illustrated by Wilson C. Dexter (1916). Both men worked independently as journalists and authors, and although their greatest success was in partnership, MacHarg is remembered for his 'The Affairs of O'Malley', tales about a tough cop which are very much forerunners of the 'hardboiled' school of crime stories.

12. THE ARCH VILLAINS

AN AFRICAN MILLIONAIRE

(Previous page) Guy Boothby's
Dr Nikola, by Stanley L. Wood.
(Above and below) Illustrations by
Gordon Browne for Grant Allen's
opening story of Colonel Clay, 'the
first important rogue in short crime
fiction', *Strand*, June 1896.

Even the best crime and detective stories would be much less than they are without the predictable villain — despite the fact that a little too many of them are somewhat similar in appearance and *modus operandi*. Sherlock Holmes' great adversaries Professor Moriarty and Colonel Moran became, naturally enough, the archetypal villains, copied in many a later mystery story, but there were others of some originality who were favoured with good illustrators and deserve a section to themselves. They were, after all, the figures in the shadows who gave the detectives their purpose in life.

There is a continuing dispute among some experts as to whether the American Melville Post's crooked lawyer, Randolph Mason, is actually the first important villain — or the slippery Colonel Clay in Grant Allen's *An African Millionaire*. The matter is difficult to resolve — indeed may finally be decided by a matter of days — as both were given to the world in 1896, Mason in volume form and Colonel Clay in episodes published month by month in the *Strand*. Perhaps the matter is really unimportant as both men are splendid rogues who should just be enjoyed in their different ways.

Guy Boothby, father of the fascinating Dr Nikola who is well represented here, also created the first gentleman crook, Simon Carne, in *A Prince of Swindlers* (1897), a forerunner of such great characters as E. W. Hornung's (1866–1921) 'Raffles', and his French rival Maurice Leblanc's *Arsène Lupin*. Leblanc (1864–1941) who was first a law student and then hack writer, scored an instant hit with his first story of the ebullient, daring and conceited Lupin. The Frenchman has many aliases and disguises, and his creator showed his own impudence and nerve when he successfully pitted Lupin against a certain famous English detective in *Arsène Lupin versus Holmlock Shears* (1908).

The villains of this era came in many shapes and as many nationalities, but as a group, those of Chinese or Oriental origin were undoubtedly the most popular. By the end of the nineteenth century the idea of the 'yellow Peril' was firmly fixed in the public mind, based partly on China's own increasing military power and her people's secret societies and occult practices. The fact that there were large colonies of Chinese in both England and America made them handy and ideal material for crime and mystery writers. Dr Fu Manchu, the creation of novelist Sax Rohmer (1883–1959), is by far the best known of these 'slant-eyed super fiends' and the stories of his battles with Nayland Smith are still highly readable. America had Wu Fang, written by Roland Daniel (1880–1969), who tangled with other criminals as well as the law, and continued to thrive even when the gangsters of the twenties made their appearance. And in the later pulps, too, there were to be few more popular villains than the Oriental.

(Facing page and above) Colonel Moran and Professor Moriarty, the two archetypal villains from the Sherlock Holmes stories, and immortalised in the *Strand* by Sidney Paget's drawings.

(Top) The first great American villain, Randolph Mason, the highly skilled and unscrupulous lawyer who uses the law to defeat the ends of justice. Created by Melville Davisson Post in 1894, the Mason stories created a furore and resulted in widespread law reforms. Picture by William Dixon.

Three pictures by Stanley L. Wood, the best of the illustrators of Guy Boothby's series of Dr Nikola mysteries, and another highly regarded portrait of the arch villain by T. S. Crowther from *The Lust of Hate*, 1898 **(left)**. The other pictures by Wood are from *A Bid for Fortune*, 1895, and show the narrator, Hatteras, in Dr Nikola's power, and two examples of what happens to those who cross the deadly doctor.

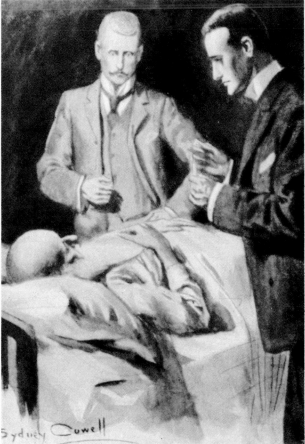

In this writer's opinion, Guy Boothby is one of the most unjustly neglected crime and mystery authors of the turn of the century, and his books, including the five Dr Nikola novels, and nearly fifty other works he penned during his short life, make exciting reading today. Boothby was born in Australia, the son of a member of the House of Assembly, but came to England in 1894 to make his fortune, and produced virtually his entire literary output in the space of the next eleven years. He was much admired by contemporaries such as Rudyard Kipling, and his books, though forgotten today, were true best-sellers in their time. Dr Nikola was introduced to readers in the *Windsor Magazine* and the pictures above were for 'Dr Nikola's Experiment' by Sydney Cowell (1899) and 'Farewell Nikola' by Harold Piffard (1901). Boothby also created the first gentleman crook in literature, Simon Carne, in 'A Prince of Swindlers' illustrated **(right)** by Edward Read (1897).

A. J. Raffles, the master cracksman and one of the most famous thieves in crime history. Created by E. W. Hornung, the cricket-loving Yorkshireman, he was seemingly destined to write detective fiction when he married Arthur Conan Doyle's sister. Raffles took up crime for the excitement and danger, and also delighted in snatching fortunes from those in whose company he moved so easily. The American artist, F. C. Yohn, provided the best Raffles illustrations for the serialisation of 'Raffles' in *Scribner's*, 1901. After Hornung's death, Raffles was 'revived' in 1932 for *The Thriller* magazine by mystery writer Barry Perowne, and turned into a two-fisted adventure **(right)**.

E. W. Hornung drew on his period in Australia in creating a mysterious bushranger with some of the Raffles qualities, called Stingaree. The exploits of this modern-day highwayman were illustrated by the Australian, George Lambert, for *Strand*, 1905.

Another exotic figure was 'Don Q', a kind of Spanish Robin Hood who took from the rich to give to the poor, and was later featured on film with Douglas Fairbanks in the lead role. The character was the creation of the much travelled Hesketh Pritchard in collaboration with his mother, and they were well served by the illustrative talents of Stanley L. Wood when 'Don Q' was featured in *Pearson's* in 1923.

Arsène Lupin-the Elusive

MAURICE LEBLANC

LES TROIS CRIMES
d'Arsène Lupin

Arsène Lupin, 'Prince of Thieves', as famous in France as Raffles in England, was a master of disguise who laughed and tormented law officers until he finally went over to their side. These three illustrations of Lupin are from English **(above)**, French **(left)** and American publications of the stories written by the former police reporter, Maurice Leblanc.

A naked man caught on board the ship he has boarded in order to uncover a criminal conspiracy, in *Scoundrels and Co,* a powerful novel of villainy first published anonymously, but later revealed to be the work of Coulson Kernahan. Picture by Stanley L. Wood (1900).

Stanley L Wood 1900

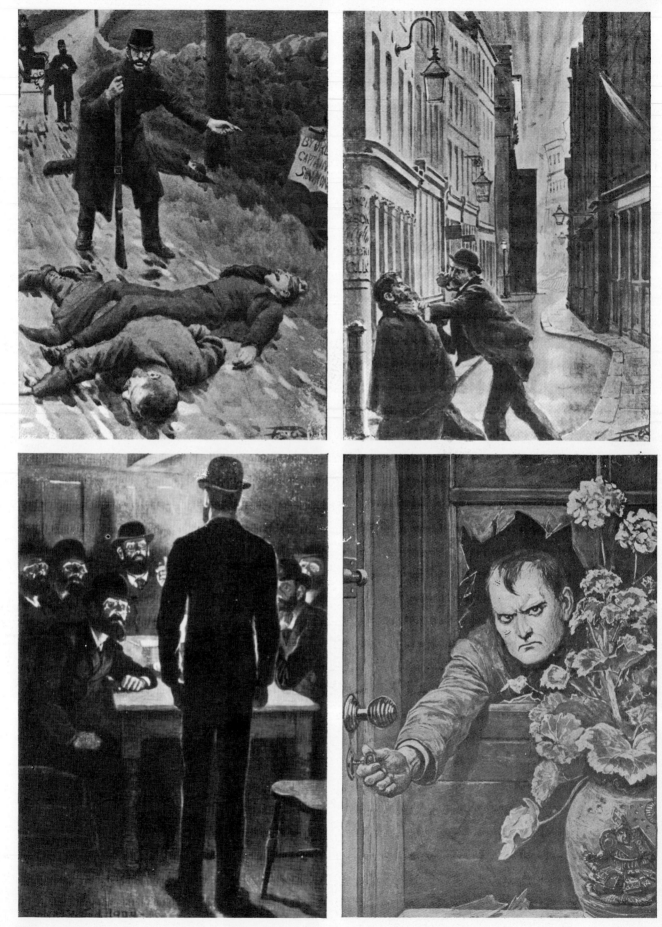

THE·COUNCIL OF·JUSTICE

EDGAR WALLACE

THE SEXTON BLAKE LIBRARY
THE LEADING DETECTIVE STORY MAGAZINE
NEW SERIES
4ᴰ

THE MOVIE MYSTERY

(Opposite) Coulson Kernahan is another forgotten turn-of-the-century crime and mystery writer, who went to considerable lengths and some danger to see at first hand the workings of the London underworld so that he could make his stories more authentic. He infiltrated anarchist gatherings to write *Captain Shannon* **(top pictures)** about a fanatical organisation perpetrating assassinations and explosions – illustrated by F S Wilson (1897). He also joined several secret societies to write *Scoundrels and Co*, 1900 **(far left)**, and sampled opium dens and other criminal haunts to get colour for what is his best book, *The Dumpling – A Detective Love Story*, 1906 **(left)**, which is actually about a modern-day Napoleon of Crime! Stanley L Wood again provides these two lower pictures.

Pictures representing four famous crime fighters:
(Top left) 'Sapper's' Bulldog Drummond making an arrest and **(right)** a pulp magazine cover featuring 'The Saint'.
(Above) Rare issue of the long-running pocket-book-sized adventures of Sexton Blake, and beside it a scarce early edition of Edgar Wallace's *The Council of Justice*.

Oriental villains were a great favourite with readers — and undoubtedly the most famous of these was the diabolical Dr Fu Manchu **(above left)**, who had untold wealth and secret forces at his disposal in his quest for world domination. The creation of an English journalist, Sax Rohmer, Dr Fu Manchu was apparently based on a shadowy figure that the writer saw in London's Chinatown.

(Above) The best-known Oriental villain after Fu Manchu was the fiendish Wu Fang who delighted in torture. His exploits were described by American thriller writer Roland Daniel, and published in *The Thriller* in the 1920s.

(Right) The tales by Thomas Burke of London's Limehouse district, where many Chinese lived, were based on personal experience, and there are many elements of crime and detection in collections like *Limehouse Nights* which this Gilbert Oakdale picture illustrated (1922).

(Opposite top) With the coming of the mobsters in America, these elements began to be reflected in stories such as 'Tarnished' by Will Rose, illustrated by Arthur Dove for *Scribner's*, 1907.

(Opposite right) 'Boston Blackie', the debonair safecracker who featured in only one book by Jack Boyle (1919) yet who has been the subject of over two dozen films.

(Far right) There were few female villains at this period — but the suitably named and very ingenious Molly Dayre who featured in Harry Harper's stories such as 'The Flying Pearls' for *Pearson's*, 1923, was an indication that things might be changing . . .

13. THE LADY DETECTIVES

(Previous page) The intrepid Flower Ross confronts deadly danger at Stonehenge in Sidney Paget's drawing for 'Followed' by Mrs L. T. Meade and Robert Eustace, *Strand*, 1900.

(Left) One of the earliest English women detective story writers was Florence Warden — actually a pen-name of Florence Price — who scored a great hit with her 'A Sensational Case', 1898, which was illustrated by St Clair Symons **(lower picture)**. She created several detectives, all of whom were men except Susie Rothley who appeared in 'The House By The Vaults', *Strand* 1905, and exposed a begging letter writer **(top)**.

Exactly twenty years after the publication of the first detective story, the world's first woman detective, Mrs Paschal, made her début in The Experiences of a Lady Detective. *Mrs Paschal relates how, suddenly finding herself devoid of means on the death of her husband, she was offered a job that was remarkable, exciting and mysterious. She accepted without hesitation, and became one of those much feared but little known persons called lady detectives.*

TAGE LA COUR and HARALD MOGENSEN
The Murder Book

Lois Cayley was one of the very first female detectives and she tackled some nefarious characters in the cases related by Grant Allen in the *Strand*, 1898. Gordon Browne provided this illustration for the unmasking of a villain in 'The Adventure of the Amateur Commission Agent'.
Not long after Miss Cayley, the beautiful Loveday Brooke made her appearance from the pen of Catherine Louise Pirkis. She was a member of a detective bureau in Lynch Court, London, and was sketched by the talented Meyer Evans (1894).

Scattered through the pages of this book are a number of accomplished female writers of detective and crime stories, but here we are concentrating on that special breed, the lady detectives. Though outshone by the men in terms of popularity, they have often demonstrated special ingenuity and a combination of clever femininity and even unladylike determination in the cause of seeing justice triumphant. These heroines of mayhem have in the main tended to be quick-witted — a decided advantage when confronted by the menacing villain of the peace — and perhaps more important still, beautiful, no mean asset when a bewitching smile and a neat turn of figure can put the evil-doer right off his evil-doings.

Among the earliest women writers of detective tales it was not uncommon to use an ambiguous pen-name or even adopt a male identity — a practice that seems to have been required by the publishers, who felt that writing such stories was not really quite ladylike. The American, Miss Emma Murdoch, for one, published much of her work as 'Lawrence L. Lynch', and another of Britain's most important writers, Mrs Elizabeth Meade Smith, was by-lined simply as L. T. Meade. Mrs Meade (1854–1914) wrote most of her 250 books for juvenile readers, but was seemingly attracted by the burgeoning detective field and created for it several important works. *The Adventures of the Amateur Commission Agent* (1898) featured Lois Cayley, one of the first female detectives; *The Brotherhood of the Seven Kings* (also 1898) was the first serial about a female gang leader; and in the various mystery-story collections she wrote with medical expert Clifford Halifax and scientist Robert Eustace, she overcame her own lack of education in such matters by utilising their knowledge to produce works that showed a fuller appreciation of the technicalities of medical and scientific detection than had been seen before from a woman.

America's most important female writer at this time was certainly Mary Roberts Rinehart (1876–1958), who devised a new form of detective story, the 'Had-I-But-Known' plot, in which a beautiful heroine plunges into one dangerous situation after another. (The flowering of this school can be seen today in the many thousands of such stories usually described as 'Gothic Romances'.) In Britain a considerable sensation surrounded the publication of *The Lodger* in 1913 by Mrs Belloc Lowndes (1868–1947) in which she captured all the horror and fear which surrounded the Jack the Ripper murders in London in 1888–89. She went on to use this clever idea of novelising famous crimes in several more works.

(Opposite) One of the first American female writers in the genre, Miss Emma Murdoch, who published all her stories under the name of Lawrence L. Lynch. These pictures by St Clair Symons are for her unusual tale *Under Fate's Wheel — a story of Mystery, Love and the Bicycle!* (*c.* 1890).

Mrs L. T. Meade, a prolific writer of stories for children and young girls, made a real breakthrough for female detective story writers. Like all women, she had received no education in scientific or legal matters, so it was difficult for such to be incorporated into her detective tales. However, she got over this by collaborating with a number of male experts in these fields and was highly successful.

(Right) With Clifford Halifax (actually Dr Edgar Beaumont) she wrote 'Stories from the Diary of a Doctor' about mysteries in a rural practice, with illustrations by Alfred Paget, *Strand*, 1893.

(Below) Her greatest triumph came in collaboration with Robert Eustace in 'The Brotherhood of the Seven Kings' which featured the reclusive philosopher Norman Head, who is in opposition to a completely new figure in detective fiction — a female gang leader who plans a series of crimes for her underlings to commit. Sidney Paget illustration for *Strand*, 1898.

(Above) Crime in the air – a case for Mrs Meade's 'Man of Science', written with Clifford Halifax and illustrated by J. Finnemore for the *Strand*, 1896.
(Right) In 1899 Mrs Meade successfully tackled a new series on her own for the *Strand*, 'Stories of the Sanctuary Club', in which she featured a Mr Bell who is called in to investigate mysteries, most of which are initially thought to have supernatural causes. **(Top)** Sidney Paget illustrates 'The Diana Sapphire' and **(below)** 'The Death Chair'.

(Left) Mrs Meade's only female detective, Miss Cusack, who tackled a series of cases in *The Harmsworth Magazine* including 'Mr Bovey's Unexpected Will' illustrated by Ernest Prater, 1896.

A novel of romance and suspense
MARY ROBERTS
RINEHART
THE BAT

DELL 0465   60c

(**Opposite**) One of the most popular American writers of detective fiction was Mary Roberts Rinehart, who scored with her first work, *The Circular Staircase* illustrated by Lester Ralph (1909). Later retitled *The Bat* and dramatised for the stage, it has kept readers enthralled until today.
Three more popular female sleuths:
(**Right**) 'The Adventures of a Lady Pearl-Broker' by Beatrice Heron-Maxwell, with pictures by Edmund J. Sullivan, in *The Harmsworth Magazine*, 1899; and (**below**) 'The Stir Outside the Café Royal: a story of Miss Van Snoop, Detective' with sketch by Hal Hurst, from the same magazine, 1898.
(**Bottom right**) Cressida, the heroine of H. B. Marriott Watson's stories, is a lawless young woman out to avenge her wronged father — and she had the distinction of being drawn by W. Russell Flint in *Pearson's*, 1907.

(Left) Two of Cyrus Cuneo's marvellous illustrations for Baroness Orczy's *Lady Molly of Scotland Yard* published in 1910.

(Above) Striking illustration for Mrs Belloc Lowndes' 'The Red Parasol', one of the adventures of Milly, Lady Member of Parliament and part-time detective – drawn by E. Verpilleux for *Pearson's*, 1920.

(Right) An early paperback edition of Mrs Belloc Lowndes' most famous work based on the Jack the Ripper story, *The Lodger*, 1913; and her eerie story of mystery, 'Too Strange Not To Be True', illustrated by Steven Spurrier for *Pearson's*, 1916.

A GREAT MYSTERY CLASSIC

THE LODGER

MRS. BELLOC LOWNDES

Some ladies in tight corners!
(Top) While Carolyn Wells' detective, Fleming Stone, is dragged away unconscious, frightful things are in store for his female companion in 'The Diamond Pin' drawn by W. Rainey for *Lippincott's Magazine*, 1919.
(Above) Ice cold water awaits the female narrator of 'Malingering' by Litton Forbes illustrated by Alfred Pearse, *Strand*, 1906.

(Bottom right) Beatrice Cressidy in the clutches of Turkish soldiers in W. Dewar's picture for 'In The Strong Man's Borders' by Frank Saville, *Pearson's*, 1909.

(Left) The cool Daphne Wrayne — with cigarette, no less! — who has numerous escapes while helping an organisation to recover property and adjust crimes in 'The Exploits Of The Adjustors' by the pseudonymous 'Valentine', *Pearson's*, 1928. Sketch by W. Bryce Hamilton.

The ladies fight back!
(Right) Maud West, the well-known lady detective, throws a good right-hander in 'Some Games of Bluff', *Pearson's*, 1926.
(Below) Detective Miss Geer proving that women can be just as brave as men, when she confronts and eventually disarms a burglar in D. E. Fife's 'The Opportunist' in *The Windsor Magazine*, 1924. Picture by Miguel Mackinlay.

139

14. THE GOLDEN ERA

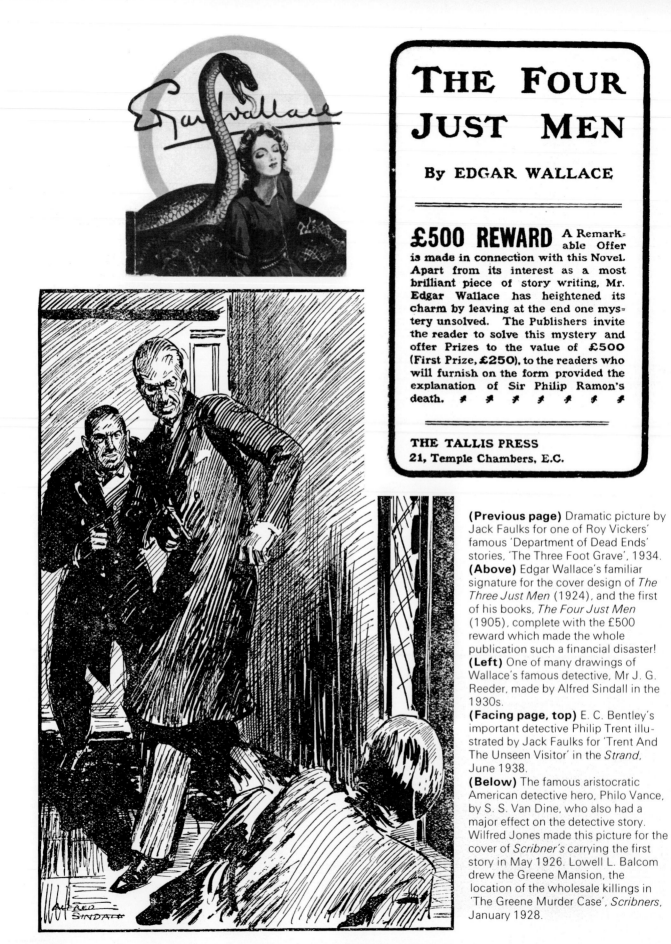

THE FOUR JUST MEN

By EDGAR WALLACE

£500 REWARD A Remarkable Offer is made in connection with this Novel. Apart from its interest as a most brilliant piece of story writing, Mr. Edgar Wallace has heightened its charm by leaving at the end one mystery unsolved. The Publishers invite the reader to solve this mystery and offer Prizes to the value of **£500** (First Prize, **£250**), to the readers who will furnish on the form provided the explanation of Sir Philip Ramon's death. ✱ ✱ ✱ ✱ ✱ ✱ ✱

THE TALLIS PRESS
21, Temple Chambers, E.C.

(Previous page) Dramatic picture by Jack Faulks for one of Roy Vickers' famous 'Department of Dead Ends' stories, 'The Three Foot Grave', 1934.
(Above) Edgar Wallace's familiar signature for the cover design of *The Three Just Men* (1924), and the first of his books, *The Four Just Men* (1905), complete with the £500 reward which made the whole publication such a financial disaster!
(Left) One of many drawings of Wallace's famous detective, Mr J. G. Reeder, made by Alfred Sindall in the 1930s.
(Facing page, top) E. C. Bentley's important detective Philip Trent illustrated by Jack Faulks for 'Trent And The Unseen Visitor' in the *Strand*, June 1938.
(Below) The famous aristocratic American detective hero, Philo Vance, by S. S. Van Dine, who also had a major effect on the detective story. Wilfred Jones made this picture for the cover of *Scribner's* carrying the first story in May 1926. Lowell L. Balcom drew the Greene Mansion, the location of the wholesale killings in 'The Greene Murder Case', *Scribners*, January 1928.

Critics are generally agreed that the period between the two World Wars was a 'Golden Age' of crime fiction. In this period the 'Modern' detective story as we know it was born — and inherent in this were several crucial developments in the genre itself. First, the stories themselves became more literate and believable, the old-style melodrama disappearing for good. Second, there was a much greater emphasis on period and character. And third, detectives and criminals functioned in a more realistic world of human frailty, error and miscalculation. The works of two important writers perhaps best summarised these changes: the Englishman, E. C. Bentley (1875–1956), and the American, S. S. Van Dine (1888–1939). Both have been separately proposed by their admirers as the 'Father of the Contemporary Detective Novel'.

Edmund Bentley was a life-long journalist and friend of the great G. K. Chesterton who influenced his work and actually encouraged him to write his famous book, *Trent's Last Case*, which Bentley described as 'not so much a detective story as an exposure of detective stories'. None the less this cunningly contrived story of detective Philip Trent was so utterly unlike any previous work that its impact was immediate and far-ranging: it has remained a highwater mark in the genre to this day. S. S. Van Dine — a pseudonym of one Willard Wright — was the man the American detective story had been waiting for since Poe. Like Bentley, he was a journalist and editor and only discovered the detective story when a breakdown caused by overwork confined him to bed for two years. Reading through many hundreds of crime books, he became convinced that he could do better, and mapped out several stories of an aristocratic amateur detective named Philo Vance. The idea was immediately accepted by *Scribner*'s magazine, and in the ensuing years Vance became unquestionably the most popular detective in America, and his creator one of the richest authors in the country, indulging himself in a variety of dilettante pursuits.

This same period also threw up one of the most flamboyant and prodigious detective and mystery writers, Edgar Wallace (1875–1932), the illegitimate son of two theatricals, who rose to a position of great social prominence and amassed huge fortunes — which he ran through with enormous extravagance and single-minded devotion to gambling on losing horses. Less obvious than Wallace, but equally important in this period, were Freeman Wills Croft (1879–1957), the creator of Inspector French; H. C. Bailey (1878–1961), who gave the British public their most popular detective between the wars, Reggie Fortune; and, of course, those two outstanding authoresses, Dorothy L. Sayers (1893–1957) with the superb Lord Peter Wimsey, and Agatha Christie (1890–1976) whose marvellous duo, Hercule Poirot and Miss Marple, need no introduction to anyone. Add to these such crime fighters as 'The Saint', 'The Toff' and 'Blackshirt', plus Sexton Blake, Nelson Lee and their contemporaries in the war on crime, and you truly have a 'Golden Age'.

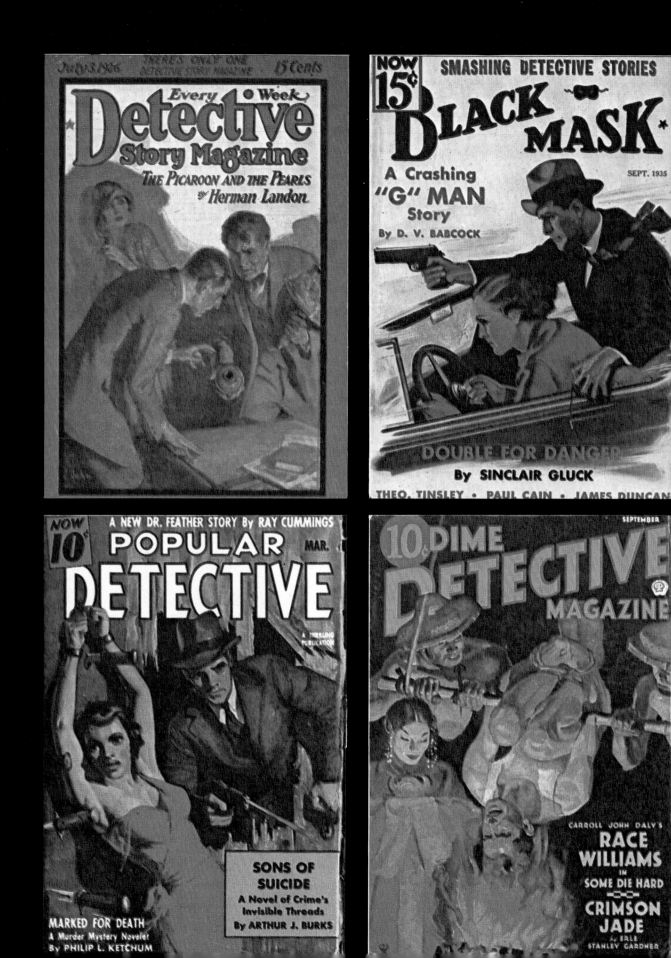

(Facing page) The four most famous detective pulp magazines: Street and Smith's pioneer *Detective Story Magazine* (1926); the legendary *Black Mask* (1935); the 'hardboiled' *Popular Detective* (1938); and the rare *Dime Detective* (1935), which featured tough, heavily-erotic stories.
(Right) A dramatic arrest for Inspector French, regarded as the first policeman in detective fiction whose methods are related step-by-step. This important figure was the work of an Irishman, Freeman Wills Croft, who took up mystery fiction while convalescing from a severe illness, and thereby gave the genre a major new impetus. Gilbert Oakdale drew the picture for 'The Greuze' (1921).
(Below right) The pleasure-loving but astute physician, Reggie Fortune, who assists Scotland Yard on its more difficult cases, and has been described as the most popular detective in England during the Golden Age. H. C. Bailey, his creator, was a newspaper correspondent and delighted in using his character as a vehicle for attacks on British attitudes. This illustration by S. A. Field was for *The President of San Jacinto* (1937).
(Below) Crime fiction begins to blow its own trumpet — an advertisement for *Convict 99* by Marie and Robert Leighton who were also responsible for creating Michael Dread, the first detective to be revealed as a murderer (1932).

The Greatest of all Convict Stories

Prison — bleak — desolate — the grim home of 400 desperate Convicts.
Into this penal settlement comes "Convict 99," reprieved from the gallows at the eleventh hour.
The powerful, undisguised story of all he went through—the agony of mind and body—the hardships he suffered before his ultimate release—makes "Convict 99" undoubtedly the finest story of Convict Life ever written.

May be had of all booksellers, price 6d., or for 8d. post free direct from The Book Publisher. PEARSON'S Book Dept. 18, Henrietta St., London, W.C.2.

Three of the most important lady writers of the Golden Age.
(Left) Margery Allingham, the creator of Albert Campion, was a varied writer of mysteries ranging from sophisticated detection to tough crime tales such as *The Mystery Man of Soho* featuring Inspector Bob Fisher of Scotland Yard.
(Below) The famous Lord Peter Wimsey by his first illustrator, John Campbell, for 'The Dragon's Head', for *Pearson's*, 1926. Dorothy L. Sayers' noble sleuth remains one of the great favourites and scarcely needs comment.
(Right) Miss Sayers' other detective, Montague Egg, the wine and spirit salesman extraordinary, in Jack Faulks' picture for 'Dirt Cheap', *Pearson's*, 1936.

(Facing page) The great Agatha Christie's two most famous sleuths, Miss Marple and Hercule Poirot, on the hunt for clues. As arguably the most popular detective story writer of the century — and certainly its best selling — the late Miss Christie jumped to fame with her first work, *The Murder of Roger Ackroyd* in 1926, and thereafter produced a new work every year until her death in 1976, her total sales said to be in excess of 400 million.

Detectives involved in the occult were highly popular between the two World Wars.

(Facing page) Two sketches by W. W. Dewar for Sax Rohmer's *The Dream Detective* (1920), tales of Moris Klaw's battle with evil forces. And

(below) Paul Toft, the detective with a profound knowledge of the supernatural, leaps into action in Kenneth Inns' picture for 'The Railway Carriage Crime', *Pearson's*, 1932.

(Right) Barnabas Hildreth, 'The Black Monk', created by the highly rated Vincent Cornier, tackles an ancient evil threatening London in 'The Mantle That Laughed', drawn by Jack Faulks for *Pearson's*, 1935.

(Below left) Hildreth investigating 'The Silver Quarrel', 1936.

(Below right) Professor Arnold Rhymer, 'The Spook Detective', searching for clues in the bizarre case of 'The Inaudible Sound' by Uel Key, drawn by A. Gilbert in *Pearson's*, 1921.

Then Hildreth gasped and pointed. "Quick —d'you see?" He touched here and there among the words.

"HAWKMAN" HAWKINS
BY FRANK SHAW

(Above) The intrepid air detective 'Hawkman' Hawkins, whose popular cases like 'The Maharajah's Jewels' (1931) took him to many exotic locations. Picture by 'Nick' for *Pearson's*.

(Below) Fidelity Dove, the beautiful but tough gang leader and righter of wrongs in Roy Vicker's tales of the same name, drawn by Jack Faulks (1935).

Roy Vickers, a long-time court reporter, also scored a major success with his stories of 'The Department of Dead Ends', a small group of Scotland Yard men assigned to seemingly impossible cases. Perhaps the best of these ingenious tales was 'The Starting Handle Murder' which Jack Faulks illustrated for *Pearson's* in 1934.

(Above) One of the first of the twentieth-century 'super heroes', Bulldog Drummond, crime fighter and adventurer *par excellence*. Created by Herman McNeile, who used the pen-name 'Sapper' — a slang term for an engineer, from his days in the Royal Engineers — the tales drew on his own experiences and ranged over many locations and tight corners, such as this example, *The Pipes of Death* (1921) illustrated by Howard K. K. Elcock.

(Left) A more traditional mystery story by 'Sapper', 'Pete Jobson, Criminal' from *Pearson's*, 1918.

(Facing page) Roger Sheringham, the likeable and unpredictable detective created by Anthony Berkeley, in a spot of trouble in *The Avenging Chance* illustrated by G. Fitzgerald in the 1930s. The publicity-shy Berkeley also wrote under the names A. B. Cox and Francis Isles and made a significant contribution to the genre with his urbane heroes.

Leslie Charteris, the man who gave the world Simon Templar, 'The Saint', based his hero's appearance and attributes on his own, and had led an adventurous life with a variety of jobs on which he could draw. The first Saint book, *Meet the Tiger*, appeared in 1928, but it was not until the 1930s that their fame began to grow and Charteris' own star was launched. On these pages are a selection of the many interpretations of 'The Saint'. **(Above and below)** The artist who drew these pictures for *The Thriller* magazine, in which Simon Templar's adventures first appeared, is unknown. The top illustration is from *The Return of the Saint* (complete with the luckless Inspector Teal) and the lower, *The Saint in New York*, both 1937. **(Left)** S. Tresilian drew this debonair Templar for 'The Legacy', *Pearson's*, 1936; while **(right)** Graves Gladney showed the crime-buster in a more typical pose in 'The Saint's No Angel' for the American *Popular Detective*, 1938.

155

More of the super crime fighters.
(Above) The prolific John Creasey's 'The Toff' was a popular figure in *The Thriller*, making the front cover in July 1935 for 'Murder of a Tramp' in which he battled with some fiendish Orientals.
(Below) An early picture of 'Blackshirt', the masked gentleman cracksman who starred in over a dozen stories by Bruce Graeme, including 'Winner Takes All' from *The Thriller*, 1935.

(Top and left) Norman Conquest, the happy-go-lucky crime-buster, takes on 'The Man Who Glowed In the Dark' by Berkeley Gray in *The Thriller*, 1938.

(Above) Tiger Standish, Sidney Horler's adventure hero in the Bulldog Drummond tradition, roamed the world in search of trouble.

Sexton Blake, who has been called 'the most famous Englishman in the world', was created by Harry Blyth in 1893 and has since appeared in over 4,000 tales written by nearly 200 writers. Blake, with his assistant, Tinker, and bloodhound, Pedro, had their first home in *The Union Jack* **(right)** and then *Detective Weekly* **(below)** before earning their own monthly magazine.

NELSON LEE. — The hero of many stirring adventures, he is as well known in the detective world as a remarkably astute crime investigator as that of the most deservedly popular Housemaster St. Frank's has ever had. No man could have a stauncher friend, nor no wrong-doer a deadlier enemy than in Nelson Lee. He came to St. Frank's at the same time as Nipper, who was his assistant at Gray's Inn Road, where the two were associated in tracking down some of the most notorious criminals of our time. In the series that has just concluded in this number, Nelson Lee has at last brought an end to an organised conspiracy to remove Dr. Stafford from the Headmastership. It nearly came off, and Nelson Lee, who supported Dr. Stafford, was for once in a way unpopular with a large section of the boys. In fact, the Head and Nelson Lee left St. Frank's in disgrace. Now that the truth is out, everyone welcomes their return to the school, especially Nelson Lee, and we publish his portrait in this issue of the Mag, in honour of the occasion.

(Above) Sexton Blake, as the hero of more novels and stories than any other detective, had several changes of image, as these two examples show: *Detective Weekly* (1934) and *Sexton Blake Library* for June 1963 – the sleuth's final appearance.
Three of Blake's rivals in the popularity stakes: **(Top)** Dixon Brett, many of whose adventures were chronicled by the stylish Jack Wylde; **(above)** Dixon Hawke, who originated from the Dundee 'fiction factory' of D. C. Thomson; and **(left)** Nelson Lee 'the master criminologist' who with his boy assistant Nipper operates at a school, seemingly the object of every criminal and evil mastermind one can imagine!

159

15. THE HARDBOILED DICKS

The private eye could only have happened first in those years after World War I, the years of Prohibition. There had always been aggressive, straight-shooting fiction heroes. But it took the mood of the twenties to add cynicism, detachment, a kind of guarded romanticism and a compulsion towards action. The disillusionment that followed the war, the frustration over the mushrooming gangster control of the cities, affected the detective story as much as it did mainstream fiction.

RON GOULART
An Informal History of the Pulp Magazines

In this final section we have come to the last important development in the detective story genre — the emergence of the private eye, or 'Hardboiled Dick' as he was more popularly called, in the pages of the pulp magazines between the two World Wars. These gaudily covered magazines printed on rough wood paper were published in their millions during this period, and there were as many different titles as there were topics to cover — romance, sport, western, war, fantasy, science-fiction and, of course, crime and mystery. That crime and mystery should produce at least as many titles as the other genres is indicative both of their popularity and of the importance of the figures who were to emerge in their pages. It has been said, and with some justification I think, that the reason why the pulp detectives were so popular was that the average American had lost faith in the society in which he or she lived, and therefore needed heroes who cared about real values — even if they were only in the pages of magazines.

Today, it is easy for anyone glancing at the lurid covers of these publications to dismiss them as trashy; closer investigation will reveal that they were the breeding ground of some of the most important talents in the modern American detective story field: for instance, Carroll John Daly (1889–1958), creator of Race Williams, the first 'Hardboiled Dick'; Dashiell Hammett (1894–1961), who epitomised this whole school of tough-guy writing and based his famous 'Continental Op' on his own days as a detective; Raymond Chandler (1888–1959), who developed the famous investigator Philip Marlowe; Erle Stanley Gardner (1889–1970), who graduated from the pulps with his unbeatable lawyer Perry Mason to become one of the best-selling writers of all time; and many more. There were, too, the famous super-heroes like 'The Shadow' who have also long outlasted their pulp origins.

The magazines ranged from the important ones such as *Black Mask* (started by the society editor, H. L. Mencken, when he was hard-up, and despised by him when it became successful) and Street and Smith's pioneer *Detective Story Magazine*, to the openly sensational and even salacious such as *Dime Mystery* and *Spicy Detective*. They were, of course, also served by a host of writers and illustrators who were as forgettable as their work. But this has not stopped any of them becoming the subject of endless debate as to their psychological and moral effects. In my opinion they are just another manifestation of what the crime and mystery story has sought to provide since Edgar Allan Poe evolved the genre — entertainment and a puzzle for the reader to try and solve ahead of the detective. Or, perhaps, as Cecil Day Lewis has more exactly expressed it, 'Detective stories are a harmless release of an innate spring of cruelty present in everyone.'

(Above) The most famous — and also the first — 'Hardboiled Dick' of the twenties was Race Williams, the cynical, ruthless, wise-cracking character created by Carroll John Daly initially for *Black Mask* magazine. Such was Williams' popularity that it was said his name on the cover of a magazine could increase the sales by twenty per cent, and his predilections for violent action, treating women roughly and treading a fine line between crime and the law, formed the prototype for hundreds of pulp characters to follow.

(Previous page) The epitomy of the pulp magazine 'Hardboiled Dick' — *Private Detective*, November 1941.
(Facing page) The two most famous pulp magazines — *Detective Story Magazine* and *Black Mask*. Despite the style and quality of their covers, the interior art in both publications was invariably poor.

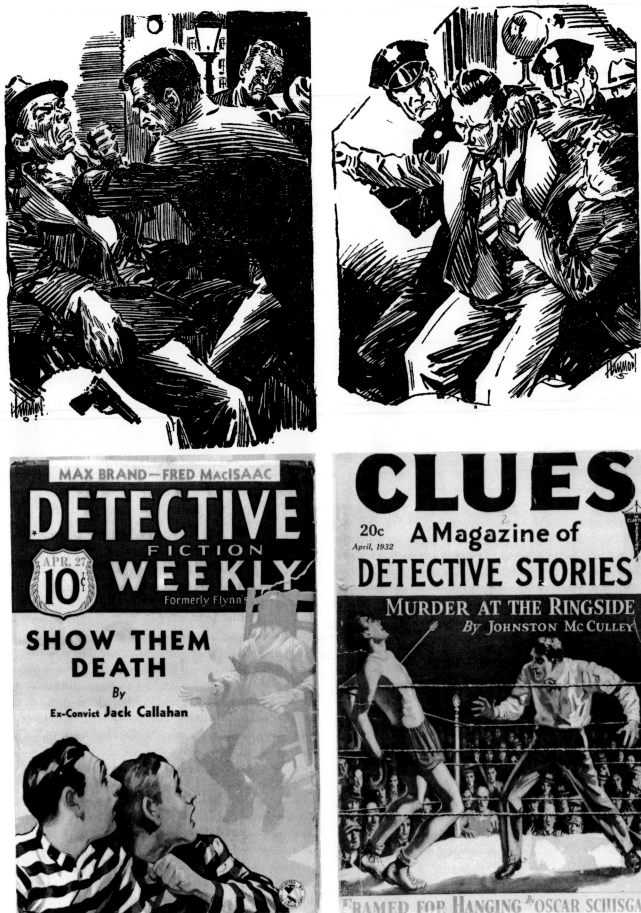

Dashiell Hammett who, with Carroll John Daly, evolved the 'Hardboiled' school, was a former Pinkerton detective who used this experience to give great authenticity to his stories of the famous Continental Op, the nameless San Francisco detective he created for *Black Mask*. Facing are two scenes from 'The Big Knockover', from an English publication of the story in 1937.

(Below) Covers of two more of the early detective pulps, *Detective Fiction Weekly*, which featured Max Brand, later to become a world-famous Western writer, and *Clues*, which went in for more off-beat tales.

(Right) Philip Marlowe, Raymond Chandler's famous sleuth, who faces many set-backs in his determination to beat crime. Despite the problems in his own life — and the loss of his beloved wife — Chandler was able to create stories ostensibly for the pulps that are still eagerly read today. Picture by Leo Summers. W. T. Ballard was another writer who rose to swift prominence in the pulps, and his stories of tough private eye Bert Daily, like this one for *10-Story Detective* (1939), had a large audience.

Norbert Davis was one of the early
pulp writers whom Raymond Chandler
said he had found influential. Davis
had begun writing Hardboiled material
while still at college, and because of
his quick success abandoned a career
in law to write. Amos Sewell provided
this picture for his story 'Paroled to
Murder', *Detective Tales*, 1936.
(Below) Covers of two rare pulp
magazines which concentrated on the
criminal fraternity, *The Underworld*
with Lyman Anderson cover (1933),
and *Gangster Stories* with art by Tom
Lovell (1932).

Other pulp magazines of the twenties and thirties ran detective tales, including *Short Stories* **(above)**, which used material by the prolific Frank Gruber. He claimed to write over 600,000 words per year and has recorded his writing life in the book *The Pulp Jungle* (1967).

(Right and below) Erle Stanley Gardner, who began his writing life in the pulps, became in time one of the world's great best-sellers and his major creation, lawyer Perry Mason, a household name everywhere. Apart from appearing in *Black Mask*, Gardner was a regular in the prestigious pulp, *Argosy*, with tales like 'Slated to Die' which got cover treatment as well as interior art by John Howett (1936).

The 'molls' always had a hard time in the pulps as these examples underline. **(Left)** Gangsters kidnapping a rival's girl in Frederick Meade's 'Murder Made Up', *Private Detective*, 1941. **(Below)** An illustration for one of the evergreen John D. MacDonald's short stories, 'Dead Reckoning', for *Detective Tales*, 1938. An Oriental mastermind drawn by J. W. Scott for *Star Detective*, 1935, and an unscrupulous businessman in the popular Frederic Brown's 'The Song of the Dead' for *New Detective*, 1940.

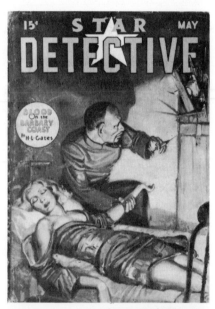

April, 1939   Vol. 4, No. 5

Towards the end of the pulp era — in the years just before World War II — several of the pulps became more openly erotic in their appeal. On this page are three leading examples. *Private Detective*, April 1939, gave clear enough indication on the cover **(top right)** and title page **(above)**, while little was left to the imagination in pictures for stories like Ken Cooper's 'Queen of Diamonds' **(top)**.

Torture of the most fiendish nature awaited detectives and girls alike in *Detective Yarns* (1939), while *Spicy Detective* (November 1942) was served by skilfully erotic artists and authors like the versatile Robert Leslie Bellem. Bellem was responsible for the Hollywood detective Dan Turner — pictured here — who eventually gained his own magazine and metamorphosed into a strip cartoon character.

169

The girls were not on the receiving end all the time, and a few even hit back at the male chauvinist pigs who used them so badly.

(Top) Anne Marsh, 'the girl Robin Hood' forced outside the law to champion the cause of robbed and ruined men, was the strikingly original creation of Arthur Leo Zagat for *Detective Tales*. Illustration for 'Daughter of Dishonour' by Amos Sewell, May 1936.

(Left) Girl sleuth on the trail in 'The Mansion of Missing Men', *Strange Detective Mysteries*, February 1942;

(middle) W. T. Ballard's 'Decoy Dame' about to extricate herself from a fix in *Ten Detective Aces*, February 1939; **(right)** a rare find in the pulps — a detective story by a woman, Betty Brooks, 'Hell to Pay in 420' from *Famous Detective*, 1942.

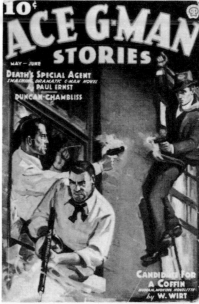

The detective pulps saw the emergence of several writers who were later to earn themselves enviable reputations in the more general fields of literature: **(Above)** The reclusive Cornell Woolrich with his hallucinatory story, 'Marihuana', for *10 Story Mystery*, 1942; **(middle)** Richard Sale, later a scriptwriter and director, who wrote hundreds of mysteries like 'There's Money in Corpses' for *Detective Tales*, 1938.

(Right) Paul Ernst, an imaginative author, was one of the best writers on the exploits of the famous G-Men, as in 'Death's Special Agent' for *Ace G-Man*, 1937. **(Below)** Robert Leslie Bellem's Dan Turner, Hollywood Detective, who led the way for the sleuth from the pulps into the comic strips.

(Above) Four panels from 'Bear Trap Kill' drawn by Max Plaisted, in which Dan is treating the girls as roughly as usual in the hunt for clues.

(Right) Queenie Starr, Dan's female Hollywood compatriot in the sleuthing business, catches a guilty party in 'Starring: A Corpse' drawn by Keats Petree. Cover and strips from the June 1950 issue.

171

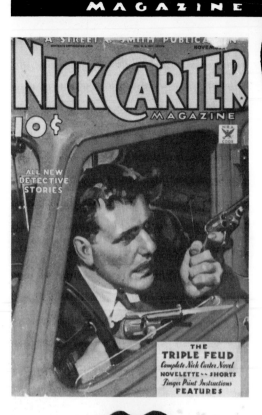

The major detective pulp 'super heroes' — still headed by the ageless Nick Carter, many of whose cases at this period were being written by Frederick W. Davis. 'The Shadow', who evolved from an American radio melodrama to become the scourge of all criminals and wrong-doers. The long-running exploits of this mysterious cloaked man were written by Maxwell Grant and were enormously popular on both sides of the Atlantic.

(Above) Another popular masked — and often cloaked — crime fighter was 'The Phantom Detective', the alias of Richard Curtis Van Loan whose adventures were recounted by Robert Wallace.

(Right) Tony Quinn, Nemesis of Crime, adopted the guise of the Black Bat in a series of tales written by G. Wayman Jones for *Black Book*

Detective in the 1930s. His winged costume was to be reflected in many later comic book heroes.

(Below) 'Crime's Indomitable Avenger' Dr Robert Clarke who led a double life as 'The Crimson Mask' and took on all manner of criminals in the stories written by Frank Johnson for *Detective Novels*.

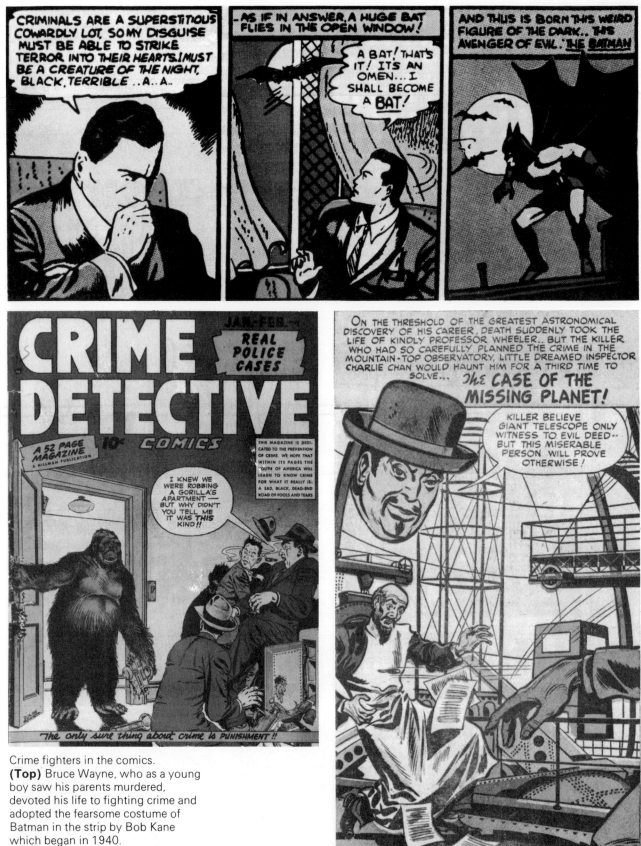

Crime fighters in the comics.
(Top) Bruce Wayne, who as a young boy saw his parents murdered, devoted his life to fighting crime and adopted the fearsome costume of Batman in the strip by Bob Kane which began in 1940.
(Left) *Crime Detective Comics*, one of the earliest and best in the field, seemed to be harking back to Edgar Allan Poe's pioneer story of the murderous ape in this wartime issue.

Dick Tracy, unquestionably the most famous strip detective, was also the first — emerging in instantly recognisable form from the brush of Chester Gould in 1931. It has been suggested his square-jawed face is an idealised conception of the looks of Sherlock Holmes, but Tracy is more a man to pitch two-fisted into any trouble — aided by some ingenious gadgets. The villains he has battled with over the years (shown below) have been a varied and often bizarre crowd, and this has proved something of a problem when the adventures have been transferred to the screen. Tracy's philosophy is summed up in the phrase that has run through this book in the actions of all those — crime fighters and criminals — represented on its pages, 'Crime does not pay.'

(Left) Charlie Chan, the Honolulu detective sergeant, whose adventures began in the novels of Earl Derr Biggers in 1925, became an immensely popular strip character and several publishing companies have run entire comics devoted to his exploits.

by CHESTER GOULD

POUCH SHOULDERS

POSIE PIGGY

UGLY CHRISTINE

JONNY SCORN

ITCHY OLIVER

SPOTS

BREATHLESS MOHONEY SCORPIO

88 KEYS THE BROW

DICK TRACY'S ROGUES' GALLERY

PRUNE FACE MOLE

MRS. PRUNEFACE SHAKEY

BRIBERY

B.B. EYES

STOOGE VILLER

MUMBLES

JEROME TROHS FLATTOP

MAMA STEVE THE TRAMP

ACKNOWLEDGEMENTS

The majority of the material in this book is from the author's own collection, but he would like to record his thanks to the following for providing extra illustrations and assistance: Ken Chapman, David Philips, John Eggling, David Alexander, The British Museum and The London Library. Also the following artists who, of course, made it all possible: Sidney Paget, Frederic Dorr Steele, H. M. Brock, Stanley L. Wood, Dudley Tennant, Cyrus Cuneo, Paul Hardy, Howard Elcock, Warwick Reynolds, Gilbert Oakdale, Margaret Brundage, F. C. Yohn, Jack Faulks, Leo Summers, Amos Sewell, John Howett, Chester Gould and many more. And not forgetting the publishers, Standard Magazines, Frank A. Munsey Company, Popular Publications Inc., Crestwood Publishing Co., Clayton Magazines Inc., Street & Smith, Conde Naste Publications Inc., Marvel Comics, Fleetway Publications and D. C. Thomson & Co. Ltd. While every effort has been made to trace the appointed owners of material still covered by copyright, for any accidental infringement please contact the author in care of the publishers.